TILE
style

TILE
style

*How to design
successfully
with tiles*

JILL BLAKE

THAMES AND HUDSON LTD

A QUARTO BOOK

First published in Great Britain in 1996
by Thames and Hudson Ltd, London

A catalogue record for this book is
available from the British Library

ISBN 0-500-01728-X

This book was designed and produced by
Quarto Publishing plc
The Old Brewery
6 Blundell Street
London N7 9BH

Senior editor Michelle Pickering
Senior art editor Catherine Shearman
Copy editors Barbara Cheney,
Maggie McCormick
Designer Roger Daniels
Illustrators Pippa Howes, Elizabeth Gray,
Keren Querfurth
Tile collages Mary Fellows
Photographers Martin Norris, Les Weiss,
Richard Gleed
Picture researchers Miriam Hyman,
Lizi Freeman, Jill Taylor
Picture manager Giulia Hetherington
Art director Moira Clinch
Editorial director Mark Dartford

Typeset in Great Britain by
Central Southern Typesetters, Eastbourne
Manufactured in Malaysia by
CH Colour Scan Sdn Bhd
Printed in Singapore by
Star Standard Industries (Pte) Ltd

CONTENTS

INTRODUCTION

Tiles, in various shapes and forms, and made from a variety of natural materials – from clay and cement to stone, marble and slate – have been both a decorative and practical building material for as long as humans have created shelters in which to live and designed specific places of beauty in which to worship a deity.

We all know of the mosaic or tessellated pavements which graced the temples, foyers, forums and houses of the ancient Romans. Many can still be seen today in sites all over Europe – they may well have been walked on for over two thousand years! But as excavations have shown, tiles were used by many other early civilizations – ancient Egyptian, Persian (Iranian), Babylonian, Moorish, Arabian, Mongol, Islamic, Chinese, Japanese – to add colour, pattern, richness and sophistication to floors and walls.

In medieval times, churches, cathedrals, cloisters and monasteries often had decorative flagged or tiled floors, the patterns of which are still as fresh and colourful today as when they were laid more than six hundred years ago. In the seventeenth and eighteenth centuries, as a result of travels made by members of the East India Company in search of furniture, fabrics and artifacts to import and sell in Europe, the decorations of Chinese porcelain began to influence those of tiles. Tin-glazed tiles in rich colours (known as Majolica tiles) became very popular, and the Dutch developed a thriving tile industry in the seventeenth century to supply the ever-increasing demands throughout Europe. They also developed their own designs, using simple hand-painted motifs of flowers, flowerpots, tulips, animals, peasant figures and rustic scenes. Blue and white became more popular than the brighter colours, and both the motifs and the blue and white colouring has become synonymous with Dutch Delftware.

In the nineteenth century in Britain and North America, designers and architects, especially those involved in the Arts & Crafts movement such as William Morris and Charles Voysey, all used and/or designed decorative tiles for floors and walls. But the most renowned tile designer of the era was a potter, William de Morgan, who started designing tiles for Morris & Co. in about 1869. De Morgan studied Persian and Turkish patterns and colours, and his tiles had characteristic flowing floral and animal motifs. Many Victorian families gathered around the statutory focal point of the home – a hearth – which was decorated with beautiful de Morgan tile panels.

Boldly decorated wall tiles and encaustic floor tiles were also being used for bathrooms, which were starting to be installed in grander houses; restrooms in gentlemen's clubs; the "health clubs" of the period – Turkish baths; and conservatories, smoking rooms and hallways in domestic, commercial and public buildings. Tiled panels were used to decorate retailers' walls where hygiene was important – dairies, butchers' shops, grocers, restaurants and bars – and they added a little cheer to institutions such as museums and city halls, libraries and other civic buildings. Once again, churches were decorated with encaustic tiles as part of the then-popular Gothic revival, as was the Palace of Westminster in London.

In the 1920s and 30s, tiles were still used in homes for fireplaces, kitchens and also by the rapidly expanding bathroom industry, where Art Deco styling was popular. However, designs and colours tended to be "safer" and less exciting than in earlier decades and rarely provided the central theme in a room. Tiles were used to much more dramatic effect in architecture – on the walls of rail stations; for the façades of stores, hotels and restaurants; to clad the exterior of modern buildings in order to provide colour and contrast to the new building materials of concrete and glass.

Today, there is a vast array of tiles available in myriad colours and patterns. In addition to the wealth of traditional tile designs which survive from centuries past, there are a multitude of modern tiles in exciting colours and shapes. All these tiles can be used creatively for floors, walls, around fireplaces, behind sinks and on countertops, as dados and dado rails. And when it comes to the way they can be arranged, it is like looking through a kaleidoscope – the permutations are endless.

You will find lots of ideas within the pages of this book which will help you create a specific style or look. You will quickly discover that designing with tiles is made easier by the fact they are usually produced to a geometric module – square, rectangular, hexagonal, octagonal, etc. Plain, attractively coloured tiles can be used simply to create a patchwork, striped or chequerboard effect. There are also infinite possibilities with patterned tiles, or with a mixture of plain or slightly textured field tiles, teamed with borders and drop-ins. They can also be used to form a border, panel or mural.

Remember that tiles do not have to be confined conventionally to the bathroom and kitchen – they are a practical alternative to wood flooring, especially in areas of heavy wear like halls. A tiled dado in a hall, porch or dining room will be an interesting and practical design feature. Or a conservatory wall can be tiled in combination with a fountain or other water feature. Tiles can form an important part of furniture design, such as a tiled table top ... anywhere where a practical, wipable, heatproof surface is required. They can also be used to refurbish old furniture – to give a new lease of life to a Victorian washstand, for example.

Wherever your personal tastes lie, and whatever your level of experience, this book will give you plenty of ideas and all the information you need to achieve the look you require, be it a sundrenched Mediterranean conservatory or a hi-tech kitchen – the possibilities are endless.

▶ This kaleidoscope of tiles shows the infinite palette of colours available and how they can be used to create stunning effects, illusions and patterns.

A HISTORY OF TILE STYLES

Mosaics can be made from clay, glass, marble, etc. Most people associate mosaics with the Romans who created stunning floors. Modern mosaics are often still arranged in traditional Roman designs.

Roman-style mosaics

The flourishing trade with the **Orient** in the 17th and 18th centuries led to the westward spread of Eastern designs and manufacturing techniques. The use of Oriental motifs and forms in Western interior decoration became increasingly popular in the 18th century, and they are still widely used today.

Traditional Gothic patterns

The Victorians, led by Pugin, loved **Gothic** designs. They were mock-medieval, heavy designs executed in rich, deep colours with intricate patterns and motifs.

Influences from the Orient

Islamic tiles have also been made since ancient times and continue to influence modern tile designers. They are best known for their rich colours and intricate flowing designs.

European nations, such as Holland, took the new techniques and designs from around the world and developed their own distinctive tiles. **Dutch Delftware** is named after the town of Delft, famous for tin-glazed earthenware. The designs, in characteristic blue and white, copied the Oriental porcelain brought to Europe by the Dutch East India Company. The traditional blue and white figurative and simple geometric patterns are still copied today.

Islamic designs

Dutch Delftware

Arts & Crafts design by William de Morgan

The **Arts & Crafts** movement, spearheaded by William Morris in the mid/late 19th century, was a reaction to heavy Victorian style and was dedicated to bringing back simple design and high standards of craftsmanship. The British artist–potter William de Morgan was a friend of Morris and became one of the most important designers in the development of ceramic tile design in the 19th century. His tiles were often used in the grand bathrooms which were being installed by the nobility and emerging middle classes, as well as in entrance halls and around fireplaces.

Art Nouveau was a decorative style popular at the turn of the century, with emphasis on sinuous flowing lines. It developed partially from the Arts & Crafts movement.

The **Art Deco** style of design became fashionable between 1910 and 1930 and was characterized by solid rectilinear shapes, and geometric and stylized motifs, some with an Egyptian flavour. In its purest form, it relied on expressive exotic features.

Art Nouveau

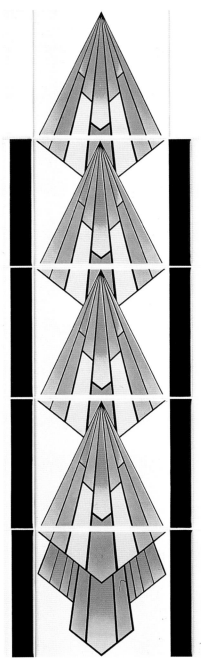

Art Deco

Modern tiles continue to develop. As new materials and production methods emerge, finishes such as the **metallic** "oilslick" lustre popular in the Victorian era can now be achieved much more cheaply. Tile designers and manufacturers often combine past production methods with modern designs and vice versa. The secret medieval method of producing inlaid tiles – **encaustics** – was rediscovered in the 19th century when it enjoyed a 70-year revival. Today, it is once again becoming popular and is used to produce both traditional and modern tile designs.

Oilslick metallics

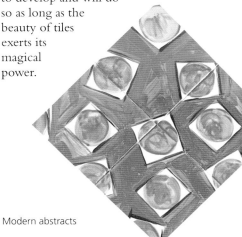

Encaustic tiles with modern designs

However, modern tile designers do not draw purely on the past for their inspiration. New, innovative styles, such as the wide choice of exciting **abstract** designs, continue to develop and will do so as long as the beauty of tiles exerts its magical power.

Modern abstracts

ROOM
DIRECTORY

HALLS

Y ou get only one chance to make a first impression, so the entrance hall – the area of the home seen initially by visitors – should be warm, welcoming and make a definite statement. At the same time it can be planned to hint at the style and colours used in the surrounding rooms. Such constructive visual links also help to make a small house or apartment seem much more spacious, especially if a similar colour is used for the flooring throughout. The hall is a transitional area, so you can be brave and bold with colour and pattern.

You can also use some visual decorating "tricks" to make a small hall look larger or one of baronial proportions seem more cosy and intimate, and to adjust the proportions so ceilings do not seem so tall, or make a long, narrow hall look less like a tunnel.

An entrance hall often takes a great deal of punishment – from dirty shoes and sticky fingers; buggy and bicycle wheels; luggage; shopping and all the things which have to be brought into or taken out of the house. So the hall is a hard-working area which needs a practical treatment for all the major surfaces – the floor, walls (especially at the side of the staircase) and woodwork.

Floors

A good interior designer begins with the floor. If you have an existing hard (permanent) flooring, consider refurbishment and repair, rather than replacement – or if this is unavoidable, call in a salvage expert to take up the old flooring as your "white elephant" might be someone else's dream product!

Choose a new hall floor treatment that is washable and hard-wearing; also consider safety – floors should always be non-trip and non-slip. In an older property, you might opt for brick, slate, terracotta *carrés,* flagstones or even reconstituted "pavers," which may come in some lovely soft ice-cream colours as well as traditional "stone." In an elegant Regency or neoclassical interior, a traditional black-and-white chequerboard floor or diamond design with black insets, possibly edged with a Greek-key border, can be created in ceramic tiles, or in marble for an extra opulent touch.

Victorian or Edwardian floors might be tiled in authentic creamy beige, terracotta, black and vivid

◄ The natural textures of rustic wood and simple plastered walls create a warm welcome in a country cottage-style hall. The contrast with the silver-blue slate floor, which has a natural vitality, gives an impression of space.

▲ The subtle contrasts in tone of the richly coloured Spanish terracotta handmade floor tiles create a warm Mediterranean look, which is enhanced by a contrasting turquoise and yellow border.

◄ A bold red and green tiled dado with raised beading and a decorative frieze suggests a return to turn-of-the-century elegance. It is offset by a black and white diamond chequerboard floor with a dramatic border which emphasizes the unusual shape.

▼ Earthenware *carrés* used to floor an entrance area are continued onto the stair treads in a typical French-style interior. Each area in the open-plan space is defined with contrasting border tiles.

◄ Terracotta tiles laid trellis fashion are bordered in black and white to define the shape of the floor.

► Mexican clay floor tiles are combined with an inset geometric pattern to provide added visual interest.

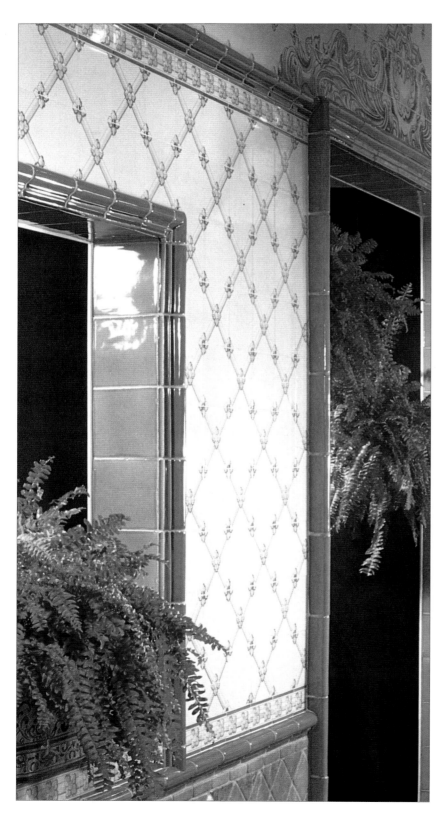

◀ Cool blue wall tiles in a trellis pattern provide an infill above a deeper coloured dado. Contrasting dado beading and borders add elegance and enhance the coordinating *trompe l'oeil* treatment.

▼ An eight-tile wide panel using different tile types shows how wall tiles can be combined to create maximum effect.

blue patterned encaustic tiles. Alternatively, interesting patterns can be created with black, terracotta and beige quarry tiles for less expense, perhaps with an encaustic tile border or "drop-in" feature tile. All these treatments need to be suitably dressed to make them easy to care for and long lasting.

If there is a stair carpet, the visual link will be strengthened if it echoes the colour and pattern of the hall floor. Where room floors meet the hall floor in doorways, use individual wooden thresholds to seal the join and paint or stain them to match the main colour. This will look coordinated, much more elegant and less obtrusive than a metal strip.

Walls

Halls, which take a lot of punishment, need to be washable – they can be wood clad, painted (perhaps using a specialist technique), or hung with vinyl wallcovering, etc. If the walls are tall, a split-level treatment can be very effective and helps to reduce the height visually. A defining plaster or wooden dado rail placed horizontally about a yard (1m) up from the floor allows for different decorating techniques to be used. For instance, apply and paint a textured surface on the area below the rail and paper the area above it with a suitable pattern.

For a really practical and unusual decorative treatment, apply ceramic tiles to the lower wall, finishing with a tiled border, nosing or dado rail. The tiles can be patterned, or plain tiles could be arranged to create a patchwork or trellis effect. In a large hall, a specially commissioned *trompe l'oeil* effect could decorate the lower part of the wall.

Colour

Look towards the warmer, welcoming end of the spectrum – rich reds, soft peach, earthy terracottas, sunny yellows, glowing golds, apricots, burnished chestnuts, exciting pinks, pumpkin orange . . . If you use a cool colour or a neutral on the floor, introduce warmer shades in the wall treatments.

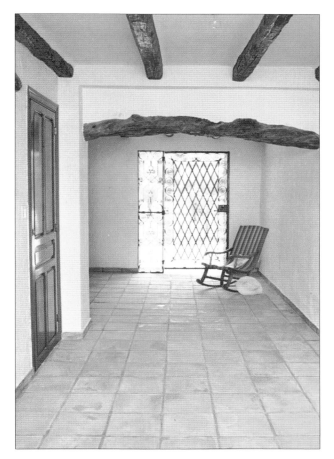

◀ A hall leading to a patio is floored with rich terracotta and buff tiles laid in a diamond pattern to enlarge the width of the floor area visually.

▼◀ Large flagstones are laid in the hall and throughout the ground floor to create visual unity in a traditional setting.

▼ A natural stone floor sets a classic, timeless theme and emphasizes the use of natural textures, such as plastic walls and wood.

LIVING ROOMS

In many homes, the living room is a multi-functional area, used by all the family for eating, entertaining, watching television, playing games or with toys, listening to (and performing) music; in other households, one room may be set aside as a family room, and the living room is used only on more formal occasions. In the former situation, the materials and furniture need to be versatile and the colour scheme practical, and all the surfaces should be robust and easy to clean. In a less-used room, the scheme can be more elegant, the colours more delicate, and the surfaces more fragile.

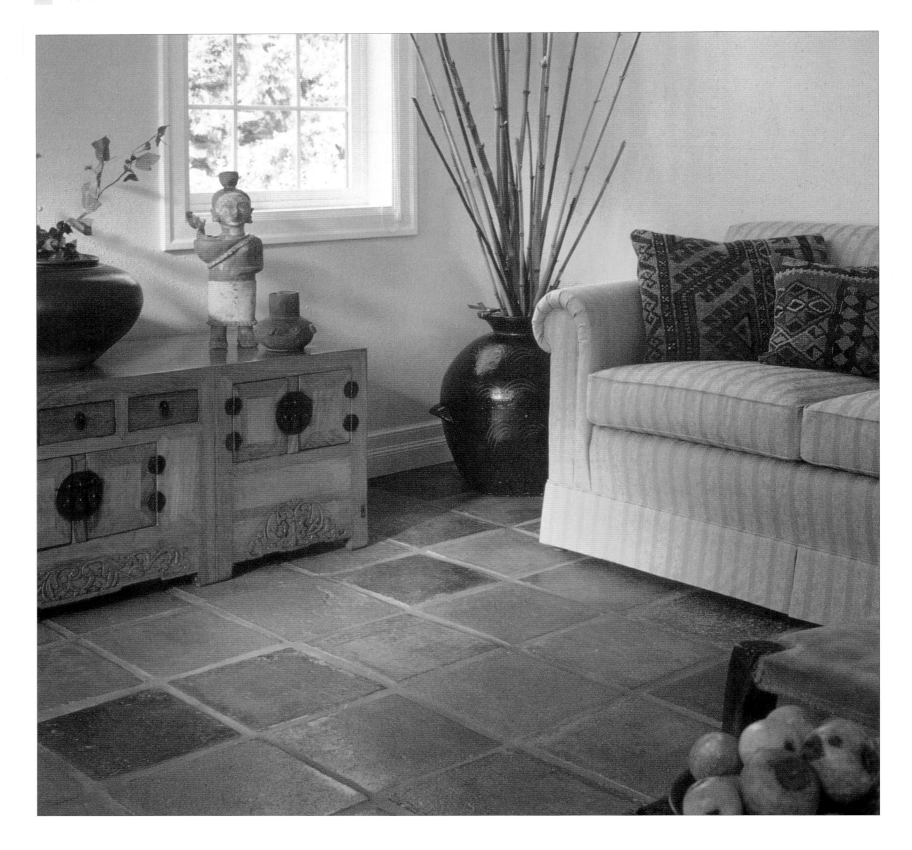

In both types of living room – functional and formal – the seating must be comfortable, the storage facilities practical, and the lighting should relate to the various uses to which the room is put. Never lose sight of the basic concept of good design, i.e. achieving a perfect combination of the practical and the aesthetic.

As one of the rooms in the home used for rest and relaxation, choose colours, patterns and textures which are as easy on the eye as they are to care for. Use middle tones for the main surfaces (the floor, walls and upholstery fabrics), restrained patterns and interesting textures. Stimulating colour accents and unusual shapes can be added in small quantities, or as accessories, to provide an extra visual dimension.

The floor gets a great deal of wear and tear in this much-used room, so aim to design from the floor up, if possible. It makes sense to choose a flooring which is hard-wearing, easy to clean, and does not show every spill and mark. Use the floor to sample and colour-match when working on the rest of the scheme.

If the living room is integrated with the kitchen or dining area, or has a conservatory, verandah or sun

◁ The terracotta flooring is taken through from the living room into the hallway to create a visual link and make the whole area look more spacious.

◁◁ Warm-coloured terracotta and bleached blonde flagstones are laid in a country-style living room and sealed to create a glowing patina.

▽ Handmade "old terracotta" tiles are individually distressed to give the impression of a well-worn floor and create a traditional, warm ambience in the working area of an elegant living room.

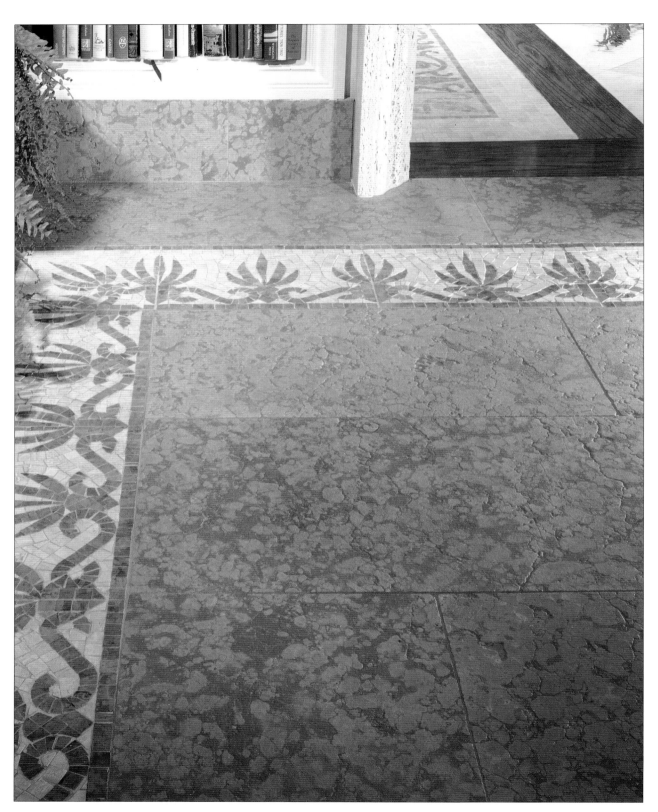

room leading from it, coordinate the various schemes and consider using the same hard flooring throughout (flagstones, quarry or slate tiles, earthenware *carrés*, brick, matt ceramic tiles, etc.). This can be softened with rugs, coir, seagrass or rush matting to help define the sitting area. Always consider safety, and make sure floor coverings do not slip or trip people, and that furniture will not slide across the floor.

Selecting a Style

First of all, consider the basic architectural character of the room in relation to the way you use the space. The size, shape, orientation and amount of natural daylight which the room receives are constraints which could dictate a suitable style – be it modern or with a specific period flavour. You may have a cherished existing item – such as a piece of furniture, fabrics, a rug or other accessory – around which you want to design the scheme. If the room is a basic bland "box," you can impose almost any style on it, as long as it is not too enclosing.

Choose the colour scheme in relation to the style as well as in consideration of the ambience you want to create. In a room for relaxation, choose pale, cool tones, work to a monochromatic theme, or use the natural/neutral range. For a more intimate, cosy atmosphere, look towards the richer, warmer colours – subtle reds, earthy terracottas, elegant rose, deep golds. If the room is small, work with the paler values of the warm colours – soft pinks, apricots and peach, pale yellows, buttercreams. Always remember the golden good decorating rule: add some cool colour contrast to emphasize the warm effect.

Focal Points

This room, more than any other in the home, needs a focal point. Traditionally, this feature was a

◀◀ Mosaics are used as a border in a library/living room in order to divide the reading and writing areas and to suggest a rug. The flooring is carried up onto the plinth of the shelves to make the area seem wider.

▲▶ The true "heart of the home" is the living room fireplace – as true now as it was in past centuries, despite central heating! Here, different tiled panels create colourful and decorative insets between the cast-iron grate and the more imposing facing. When selecting a fireplace, make sure the scale is right – an overpowering construction can spoil the balance of the room.

fireplace or stove, which is comfortable and warm to group seating around for talking, watching television, playing games or listening to music. In the summer it may be more practical to reposition the furniture so the outside becomes the focal point – choose window treatments to dramatize and enhance the view of the garden.

A fireplace, chimneypiece or stove could be the starting point for the scheme, as well as the focal point. If you install a new one, make sure it

is the correct scale in relation to the size of the room (from the heat output aspect as well as the visual aspect).

From the practical point of view, brick, stone, ceramic tiles and slate are all heat-resistant, and are a wise choice for hearths, wall areas and chimney breasts backing free-standing stoves or as an integral part of the fireplace.

Marble or carved wooden fire surrounds look classically elegant, and come in a wide range of shapes

and styles, from Jacobean and neoclassical to traditional "swagged" designs. Stone or brick-clad chimney breasts or inglenooks will be suitably rustic in a country house or cottage setting. A continental or Scandinavian-style stove can be fully tiled and set on a tiled hearth against a tiled wall area. Cast-iron or enamelled wood-burning stoves can be similarly treated and positioned on a heatproof hearth.

In a Victorian or Edwardian setting, choose a black cast-iron grate

with decorated tiled inset and hearth, and wooden overmantel. For a specific Arts & Crafts theme, try to find suitable tile designs by William de Morgan, William Morris or Walter Crane; for an Art Nouveau theme, there are tiles available in the Charles Rennie Mackintosh image. For a 1920s/30s Art Deco setting, you will need to search for a typical fully tiled fireplace surround and hearth; alternatively, you can design one using suitable geometric tiles sympathetic to the period.

◀ Bold blue and white hand-painted octagonal tiles, combined with plain blue triangles and a neat Izmir border in the 17th-century Majolica tradition, form a practical and eye-catching focal point behind the cast-iron wood-burning stove in this country-style living room.

◀ The fireplace and fireback, in Dutch Delft-tile tradition, have authentic motifs painted on the glazed tiles. Such tiles must be fireproof if they are used in an open fire. They can be combined with stoves or used as a decorative focal point and filled with plants and flowers during summer.

◀ The blue-and-white diamond tiles of the fireplace and hearth look like a handcrafted Shaker-style patchwork.

▼ Subtle grey-green tiles on the hearth and mantelpiece frame the fireplace and are combined with warm terracotta on the floor.

KITCHENS AND
DINING ROOMS

The kitchen is often seen rather romantically as the "heart of the home." This mood is reinforced with the current nostalgic trend towards the rustic, real wood, country-style kitchen — complete with old-fashioned range, ceramic sink, potted herbs, dried flowers and basketware. But it is also the main work area or nerve centre of the home. Nowadays a dining room may be part of the kitchen, or also used as a workroom or playroom. Such multipurpose areas need careful planning, furnishing and decorating.

The Kitchen

A kitchen consequently needs hard-wearing materials on floors, walls, units and countertops to provide impervious, hygienic and easy-to-clean surfaces. Ceramic tiles are a practical and decorative solution. They can be used as "splashbacks" behind cooking areas, sink and food preparation areas, and as work surfaces on units and tables. Riven slate, stone, quarry and ceramic tiles, and earthenware *carrés* are all possible floorings, which can be sealed to make them easy to care for and long lasting, and treated to be non-slip. With a clever choice of colour and texture, these treatments will not look stark or feel harsh and unyielding underfoot.

Kitchens can often be cold, clinical places, despite the hot and steamy activities which take place in them. A radiator is sometimes not installed because of the presence of an oven; however, with good insulation the appliances give off very little heat. To counterbalance the cold, look towards warmer, more inviting colours for the main surfaces – the floor, walls, ceiling, cabinets and woodwork, and window treatments; the harsh look of wall tiles can be softened with some light-filtering textures – for instance, cane, trellis, shutters, slatted blinds or sheer fabric café curtains; a rug or natural floorcovering can be used to define the floor in dining/sitting areas; place terracotta pots planted with herbs or brightly coloured flowers on available surfaces.

A warm kitchen can be cooled with a soft green, minty tone, faded Shaker blue, or a romantic lilac colour scheme. Shiny, reflective textures also have a cooling effect and help to increase the apparent size of a small kitchen.

Stylish Selection

A kitchen should be as carefully themed as any other room in the home, to give it an overall mood and

▲ The texture of warm rose Venetian marble tiles on this splashback sets off a decorative *Herbes de Provençe* inset tiled border.

▲▶ A counter of stoneware tiles is combined with a colourful French Fauve-style border, set into a white glazed splashback.

◀ A patchwork effect is obtained with hand-glazed, dragged tiles in exotic colours, hung trellis fashion and grouted in white.

▶ Highly glazed vivid blue tiles matching the range form a decorative heatproof backing inside the recess, and are bordered in unglazed terracotta tiles for extra visual impact.

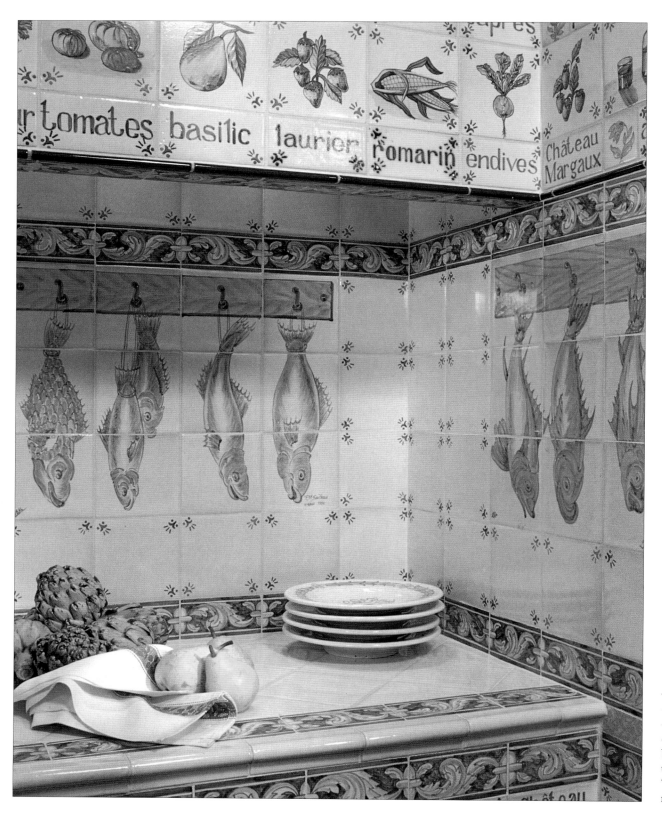

ambience. Choose the floor and wall tiles to enhance the basic style of your kitchen – rustic pavers, brick, warm terracottas, heathery quarries and continental earthenware slabs will all complement a country-style kitchen with pine, distressed or painted furniture. Display copper utensils and touches of brass to add to the warm, welcoming feel.

Add an appropriate flavour to a period scheme using specific patterns such as traditional blue and white Delft; richly coloured Arts & Crafts patterned wall and border tiles; sunny, exotic Mediterranean glazes; or flora, vegetable and fauna designs. Alternatively, combine sleek, glossy, geometric patterns on wall tiles with slate, marble, granite or terrazzo flooring (non-slip) for a more modern, minimalist scheme.

Plain wall and floor tiles can be used to great effect. Use two tones (light and dark), or strongly contrasting colours – such as turquoise blue and terracotta, red and green, yellow and lilac, black and white, brown and cream – to create a chequerboard or striped effect. This treatment can visually enlarge a small floor, especially if it relates to the colour of the cupboards, or if the baseboard (skirting) is decorated to match the floor. Or use a contrasting colour, or specific pattern, to create a border effect to help define separate areas – for instance, to divide the kitchen from the dining area, or the utility room from the kitchen, or to outline an important feature such as a recess, window frame or hutch (dresser).

On a large wall area, tiles can be cut and hung in a more unusual way – for example, set diamond-fashion on a dado. Panels could be created on a big, blank area for different effects – for instance, a mural could be painted in the centre panel; or tiles could be arranged to suggest a "room-with-a-view" where there is no window; or a softly graduated

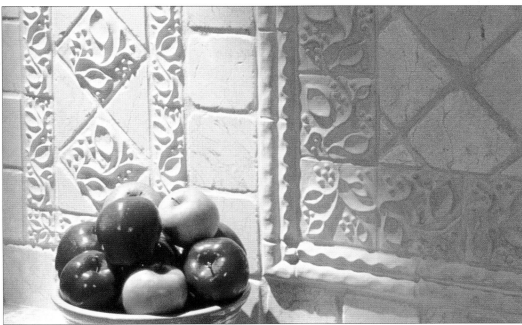

▲ This kitchen in classic blue and white has wooden counters and a related tile splashback.

◄◄ Tiles of fish, fruit and border are combined to form a practical counter for food preparation and visual interest in a windowless area.

▲ Heavy relief decoration on glazed tiles in white and soft neutrals adds textural interest to an area. Neutral tiles give flexibility to the overall colour scheme.

◄ Plain terracotta and navy-blue tiles are hung to create a subtle horizontal striped effect, enhancing a country kitchen style.

monochromatic effect could be created using tiles in different tones of one colour (start with the paler values of the colour at ceiling height and work down to the deeper tones at floor level).

A plain or dull tiled wall can be enlivened by using a different or unusual coloured grout, instead of the conventional white or beige, or "background to the tile" colour – for instance, strong yellow with plain white tiles; deep green with pale pink or beige; royal blue with apricot or peach; terracotta or deep Indian red with pale green or soft yellow. However, charcoal grey or black tiles can look stunning grouted in white. Some coloured grouts are available ready-mixed, or you can mix your own.

The Dining Room

The style, pattern and colour scheme for a dining room depends to some extent – like the kitchen – on the meals you serve, and the type of cooking and entertaining you do. As with all successful decorating, consideration needs to be given to the size, shape, orientation and the architectural character of the room but aim to create a cosy, intimate ambience.

Nowadays a dining room may be a part of the living room or kitchen, or it may have to double as a study, workroom or playroom. Such multipurpose areas need very careful planning, furnishing and decorating if they are to be functional as well as elegant. The dining area should echo the style, colour scheme and theme of the rest of the room.

If you have a separate dining room which is mainly used for more formal entertaining and important family gatherings, aim to make it really special. Give it a distinctive style or period flavour which is warm and inviting, to encourage family and guests to enjoy and linger over a lovingly prepared meal.

◄◄ African slate flooring in warm buff, burnt-orange and grey contrast with the shiny black granite counters and the range which also acts as a foil for the wooden cabinets.

Chairs should be comfortable, with practical (washable) covers, and of the correct height to relate well to an ample table (i.e. plenty of space for diners' knees and elbows). There should be adequate storage for glasses, china, flatware (cutlery), linen and other dining table items, and heatproof food-serving facilities.

Choose appetite-inducing colours from the warmer side of the spectrum, such as deep wine or burgundy reds, rich rose, sugar pinks, earthy terracottas, glowing yellows and golds teamed with gleaming mahogany or waxed pine; or more subtle ice-cream colours, such as strawberry, raspberry, peach, apricot, lime or citron teamed with cream and a little pistachio or herb green.

Brighten up a dark dining room with sharp lemon, warm gold or sunflower yellow, spiked with white and contrasted with sky blue or grass green to suggest sunshine and the

▲ An all-tiled kitchen – floor, walls, countertops, cabinet recess – creates a subtle country effect in a small apartment kitchen. The floor pattern expands the space visually.

◄ An elegant kitchen, with a riven slate floor in coordinating shades of grey and blue, provides a cool ambience for cooking, washing and other hot and steamy activities.

▷ This scheme relies on rustic textures, sharpened with copper and opalescent glass, to provide visual contrast. The subtle colour of the tiled area around the stove makes the scheme less obtrusive.

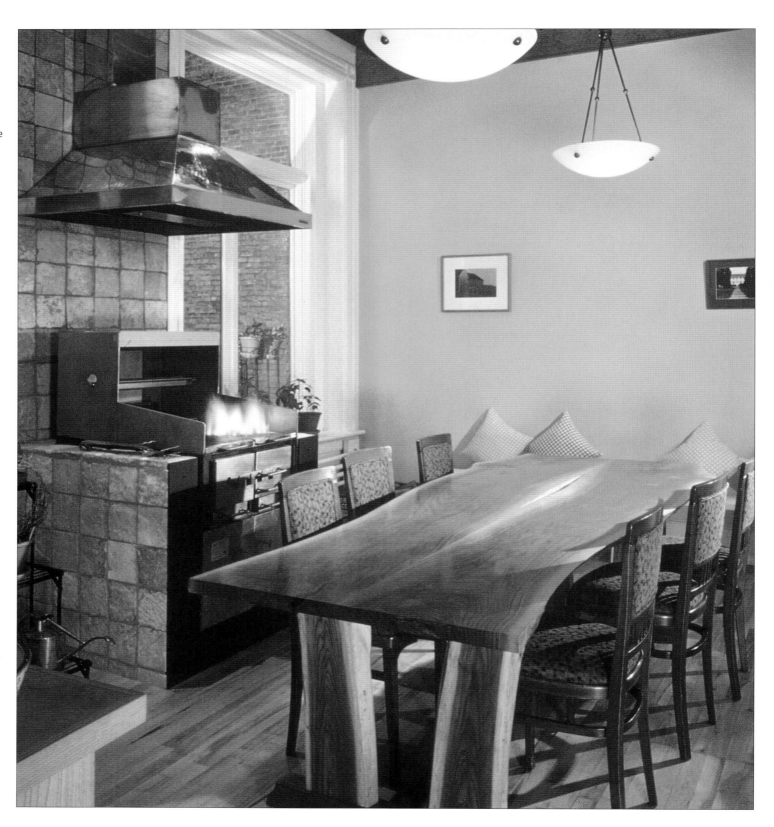

warmth of long summer days. In a large space, red and green, or a gold and red scheme, can help to set a Scottish theme, especially if tartan plaid or checks and suitable accessories are selected.

Stylish Schemes

Dining room styling can be modern, simple and streamlined. The warm, rich, earthy colour and rustic textures associated with the currently popular Mediterranean look will suggest meals eaten *al fresco* in Provence, Tuscany or on a Greek island. To emulate, combine a deep blue ceiling with a terracotta-tiled floor and introduce some yellow ochre to contrast – for an outdoor look, stencilled vine leaves or bunches of grapes could echo the pattern on a tiled table top or wall area.

For a sleek Scandinavian or minimalist modern style, use teak or light wood furniture, creamy neutral colours and natural textures combined with colourful accents in china and glassware. Soften the floors with shaggy non-slip rugs. For a more Metropolitan mood, combine black ash furniture with a grey granite table top, black and white

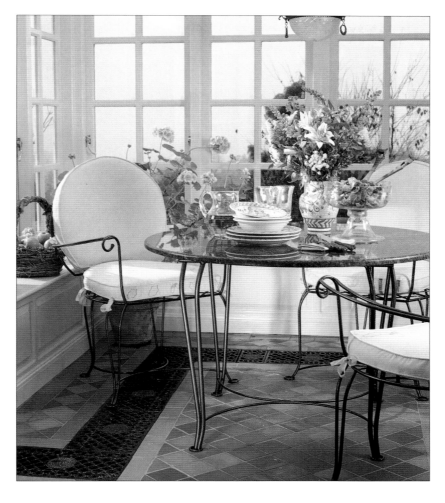

chequerboard tiled floor, and again some colourful accessories to lighten the scheme.

For a traditional look, opt for a specific period flavour. A Georgian, colonial or Regency theme is very popular for dining rooms, partly because there is so much good dining furniture available in yew, mahogany, and light and dark oak. These woods look good teamed with rich textures and enhanced with warm reds and golds and touches of brass, and with Oriental rugs or rush mats on flagstone floors.

To create a country cottage ambience, a golden pine scrubbed table and waxed sideboard combined with distressed or painted furniture in slightly faded "Shaker colours" (i.e. denim blues and grey-greens) can be set on a burnt-orange quarry-tiled or earthenware slabbed floor.

For an Arts & Crafts look, team a limed or light oak refectory table with a matching sideboard, tall-backed rush-seated chairs and authentic William Morris wallcoverings and/or fabrics. A traditional fireplace could be the starting point for such a scheme, with cast-iron grate and tiled inset.

A Practical Approach

Surfaces in a dining room must be easy to clean as occasional spillages are unavoidable. Walls may be splashed when bottles are opened and food served. To be really practical, surfaces need to be heatproof – a ceramic-tiled top can be a boon on a unit, sideboard or serving table. A matching tiled "splashback" for the wall behind the serving area is a feature worth considering. If it fits the style of the room, a capacious Victorian or Edwardian washstand with tiled or marble top and back can be a practical alternative.

The floor should be equally practical, and preferably washable. The suggestions outlined for kitchens are all applicable for a dining room.

▶ A 17th-century-style dining room in a country house with rich, dark wood furniture is enhanced by reclaimed French terracotta floor tiles and warm pink colour-washed walls.

▲ A terracotta tiled floor is used for a conservatory dining area. The border detail defines the space, and the floor provides good colour contrast with white walls/furniture.

CONSERVATORIES

Some houses have a conservatory, sun room, porch, gazebo or verandah as part of the architecture. Those built in the eighteenth or nineteenth century (or at the turn of the century) may already have a fabulous floor – highly decorative encaustic tiles or flagstones were often laid in such areas; quarry tiles in terracotta, beige and black; brick pavers; or even traditional black and white marble in the grander properties. If it is necessary to do a little refurbishment of such an existing floor, call in an expert to help restore it to its former glory.

However, if this type of floor is not to your taste, a salvage expert can remove it and sell it to somebody else, giving you some extra budget to put towards a new floor.

When considering flooring for conservatories, porches, verandahs, etc., bear in mind that it needs to be impervious to damp and easy to clean – there will be drips from plant watering and mud tramped in from outside. The surface could be continued onto the patio, or down the front walk (path) to the gate – a fashion in former times – to create continuity and a visual link.

It is wise to choose a frostproof quality tile, slate or stone, since the floor can become very cold in winter, especially if it has absorbed water – a strong shaft of sunlight, magnified by a glazed roof or large window, shining onto a very cold floor can cause it to crack. If the surface is porous, it needs to be adequately sealed to protect it from the elements.

Master Planning

Most conservatories, porches, verandahs, etc., are an extension to the main house, built to provide extra living space and other facilities; porches and some verandahs are incorporated to enhance the entrance and cut out drafts. If you wish to add an extra room, plan the use of space carefully, working out exactly what function you wish the area to perform, and then furnish and equip it accordingly.

If a conservatory or sun room is to contain exotic plants, and be partially used as a greenhouse, it will need carefully controlled ventilation, sun screening, and possibly automatic watering facilities. Glazing should always be double, and in some cases triple, and in vulnerable situations – such as when the extension is used as a playroom – use special shatter-proof laminated glass to avoid accidents.

However much glass is used in the construction of such an extension,

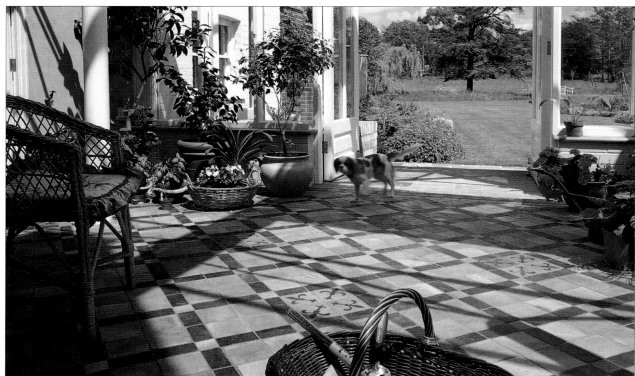

▲ A small conservatory dining room is floored with antique yellow terracotta tiles laid with dark slate keystones to create an illusion of greater width.

◀ Traditional terracotta tiles have been personalized with a stencilled decorative pattern and fleur-de-lys motif.

▶ Octagonal Mexican terracotta tiles with square inset provide warmth and textural interest all year round. The upholstery echoes the colour and shape of the floor tiles.

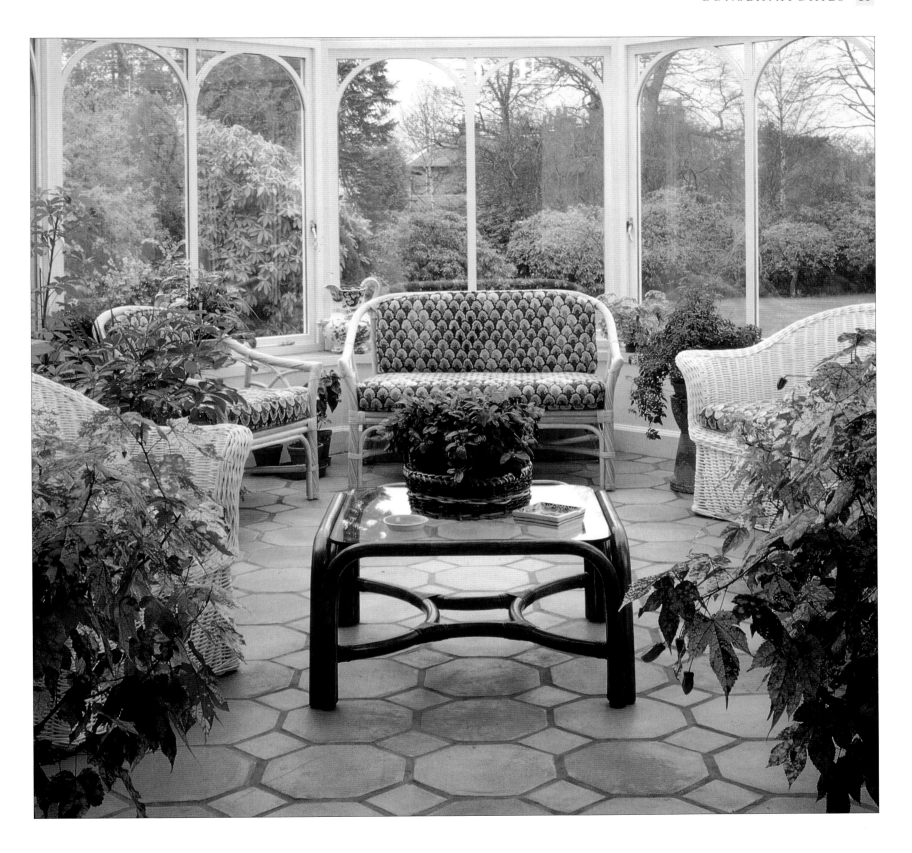

light will always be lost from the adjoining area. To counteract this, decorate both the extension and the adjoining spaces in pale or sunny colours and include some light-reflecting surfaces. As for any room, a coordinating theme used throughout creates an impression of unity and spaciousness, especially if the floor is the same or a similar colour.

Conservatories, verandahs and sun rooms can be styled and furnished as carefully as any other room. A "return to the Raj" look can be created by using neutral colours and natural textures, with cane or wicker furniture, ceiling fans, slatted wooden or rattan blinds under sheer drapes, and terracotta floor tiles or brick pavers, all enhanced by suitable

plants and colourful containers to provide accents.

For an extension intended mainly for family living or dining, consider a Regency theme – delicate white wrought-iron furniture and stone floors offset with rich reds and golds; or a neoclassical style, with black and white tiled floor, elegant pillars, Wedgwood blue walls and ceiling,

and touches of terracotta and black. A successful Gothic look requires suitable fenestration – tall, slim windows with pointed tops – and introduce a glass-topped table on black iron trestles with matching black iron chairs and accessories, including curtain poles and candle and light fixtures. The colour scheme can be mainly a grey monochromatic

◀ This exotic Moorish-style indoor atrium is decorated in discreet neutrals. The antique *blanc rose* terracotta floor with antique barr cabochons acts as a foil to the richly coloured furniture.

▲ A classic clay fountain (the faucet makes plant watering easier) framed with decorative glazed Moroccan tiles is set against a background of white mosaics.

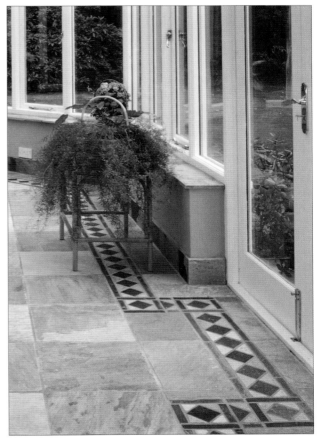

◀ A fully glazed conservatory can be used to raise plants and bonsai trees, as well as for summer dining. The pale terracotta blinds echo the colour of the earthenware floor tiles.

▼ This Gothic-style conservatory has a stone floor with inset diamond border design to emphasize the shape of the room.

one, accented with scarlet, purple and mauve. Or for a more modern, minimalist setting, choose stream-lined Italianate furniture in chrome and glass, enhanced by a neutral colour scheme and primary accents.

When the space is to be specifically used for dining, you might prefer an *al fresco* Mediterranean theme. Aim to echo the look of open-air sun-baked patios and tile the floor with earthenware *carrés* in rich burnt-orange; paint walls with an ochre glaze over white-painted brick; and bring in a strong bright or sky blue to contrast. Introduce some pictorial ceramic wall tile panels to create an impression of a view, and accessorize with suitable plants and vines – these could be trained to form a sun canopy overhead.

Pictorial tiled wall treatments also come into their own in pool houses and games rooms – these could be specially commissioned to follow a specific theme. Traditional patterned terrazzo flooring, stone or brick are all warm and safe to walk on (floors surrounding pools must be non-slip), and sunshine colours of yellows, golds, terracottas, peach and buttermilk, combined with brilliant blue, will add warmth and elegance.

Utility Rooms

Utility rooms usually lead off the kitchen, porch or conservatory, and are the area of the home which takes the most "punishment" of all. Its practical uses are endless, varying from repotting plants or growing seedlings, to scouring pots and pans. This area may also contain the freezer, cupboards and racks for long-term vegetable and dry goods storage, a washing machine, dryer and ironing equipment, etc. It may also double as a hobby area and be the only place in the house to store tools.

The floor should ideally be easy to scrub and mop, and be impervious to spillages, breakages, and muddy paw and foot marks. Choose a permanent "hard" surface in a practical middle-tone colour. Many of the floorings suggested for kitchens are equally suitable for a utility room – for example, riven slate, flagstones, non-slip ceramic tiles, quarried or reconstituted stone slabs, brick (sealed), earthenware *carrés* and quarry tiles.

Apart from cupboards, shelves and racks, etc., there should be adequate drainers and work surfaces – especially to either side of any (deep) sink – and a generous-sized table. If space is short, consider a butcher's block on wheels or a folding or drop-down-flap table – or one which pulls/folds out from a storage unit. Again, the surface should be easy to clean, and scrub if necessary, so some of the suggested floorings can be used as countertops and splashbacks, creating a feeling of continuity. Make sure any grouting is hygienic and impervious to cooking liquids, acids, etc.

Choose colours to contribute to the visual link between the utility room and the room from which it leads. Warmer tones will soften and take the chill off a rather clinical and utilitarian area, which may be filled with fairly harsh textures and shiny surfaces. Patterns and colours can also be bolder in this room – it is a good place for a stimulating scheme – perhaps using complementary (contrasting) colours, or a neutral colour with very bright accents.

◀ A simple glazed extension creates a sunny summer living room. The classic white tiled floor with black key square insets is enhanced by the colourful rattan furniture; white vertical blinds form an adjustable sunscreen.

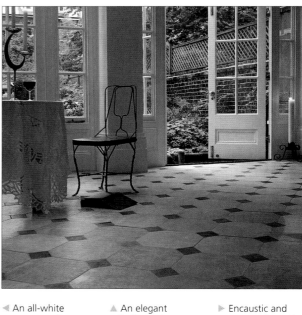

◀ An all-white conservatory is floored with soft blue-grey slate slabs laid at an angle to expand the area visually.

▲ An elegant Palladian-style garden room is floored with classic limestone flagstones and faded blue insets.

▶ Encaustic and geometric floor tiles recreate the original 1860 tiled conservatory floor at the prestigious Hurlingham Club in London, England.

BATHROOMS AND BEDROOMS

The bathroom, downstairs "powder room" and shower room are utilitarian areas of the home which are often cold and clinical and rather uncomfortable, and generally not as carefully styled as other rooms in the home. But as modern plumbing becomes more efficient and we develop sybaritic tendencies, the bathroom is being filled with more complex equipment and is now a room in which to enjoy oneself. It may also be converted to a dual purpose fitness and personal hygiene room. Bedrooms are usually highly personal spaces and can be decorated and furnished in a more individual way than other rooms.

The Bathroom

Unless you are doing major building, refurbishment or conversion work, the bathroom is usually the smallest room in the house and needs careful planning in order to fit everything in, and clever colour scheming and decorative treatments to make it appear more spacious. Mirrors and mirror tiles help to magnify space and reflect both natural day and night time artificial light. Mirrors and mirror tiles must be hung on a perfectly flat surface to avoid distorted reflections – rough walls can be clad with special wall or plasterboard first, or the tiles can be mounted onto chipboard or hardboard panels.

Comfortable Colours

Bathrooms tend to be cold because there are so many clinical surfaces and shiny textures. The bath, basin, shower tray/stall, toilet, etc., are all designed to withstand dirt and damp, and the form of these items is often harsh and unyielding. Gleaming chrome taps and rails, glossy white ceramic tiles (or shiny cold marble), enamelled cast-iron baths, and glass shower screens all add to this unwelcoming impression. Soft textures will offset these light-reflecting ones – for instance, fluffy bath towels and mats, possibly trimmed with embroidery or crochet; lace, gauze or other sheer fabric for curtains or blinds; baskets filled with soaps and other toiletries; plants chosen for their steam-loving properties and for variation in shape and texture.

In a small, dark windowless bathroom consider creating a *trompe l'oeil* effect with a tiled panel suggesting a view or seascape; or use a mirror or mirror tiles to simulate a window and "dress" it with curtains or blinds subtly lit with concealed pelmet lighting.

Choose paler tones of colours, or a monochromatic (one-colour) effect to enlarge a small space visually. Use stronger colours in a bigger room, or some bold contrasts for a more stimulating atmosphere (in a busy bathroom, where you want to encourage fast throughput!) – for maximum effect, mix complementary (contrasting) colours.

To create a warm and welcoming bathroom, the sunshine colours – pale yellow, apricot, dusty brick, soft coral and faded gold – teamed with warm whites, and accented with some brilliant sky blue, will create a summery feel all the year round. Alternatively, combine coffee with creams and terracotta, sharpened with strong jade green; or look to a floral theme for inspiration, such as the crisp pinks, soft mauves, golden yellows and creams found in a bunch of freesias, cooled down with soft spring green.

Careful Coordination

The starting point will probably be the existing colour and style of the sanitaryware (bath, basin, toilet, etc.) which is already installed. Accurate colour-matching is essential; you must look at proposed materials in the bathroom under exact lighting conditions. The sanitaryware may be a cold colour – for example, "pampas" or "whisper" greys and greens, or even blue; other popular colours in the past include burgundy red, tan-orange, very dark blue, and even black. These are all very difficult bathroom colours as, contrary to

▷ A stunning custom-designed shower room: the *trompe l'oeil* effect is created using glass mosaics.

◁◁ A recessed sink in a large bathroom is adorned with flowers. The vanity unit is tiled in coordination with the wall tiles and with the pattern on the basin.

◁ A mirrored alcove forms a decorative focal point in a bedroom. Patterned and plain tiles create a "frame" for the mirror and provide an attractive display shelf for personal items.

popular belief, they show up every mark as an unappealing grey scum.

A strong-coloured set cannot be toned down or hidden by combining it with safe neutrals. The only way to detract from an anti-social, bright colour is to use a very bold treatment which "shouts back at it," or to create a monochromatic scheme using the suite colour as the darkest tone. Pick a wallcovering or tiles which incorporate the main colour but also introduce some strong contrasts. Echo these colours in your window treatments, flooring and accessories.

If you are lucky enough to be starting a bathroom from scratch, choose sanitaryware which allows for flexible styling and has future design and colour scheming possibilities. White is a classic choice and has endless possible schematic permutations, although it can be cold; some of the ivory, champagne and soft "blush" colours will be equally easy (and warmer) to work around. Or consider a sharper pastel – lilac is sometimes a popular colour for bathrooms and can be the basis for a really elegant scheme.

Many bathroom sanitaryware producers have a marketing arrangement with ceramic wall and floor tile manufacturers, so it is fairly easy to find tiles to coordinate well with the ceramic pieces if you want a more subtle scheme. Bear in mind that the tiles and the sanitaryware will be with you for a long time to come, so do some very careful

sampling before reaching a decision. If the tiles are patterned, make sure that the overall effect will not be too overpowering in a small space – or that the design will not appear to be sliding off the wall when completely tiled! Look at as many tiles side by side as possible; pictures and leaflets are also useful as a guide to the overall effect, but do not rely on them for accurate colour matching.

If a bathroom and bedroom are *en suite*, aim to create a visual link between the two rooms. Carry some colour through from the bedroom into the bathroom (or vice versa)

with the same, or a similar colour, on the floor; choose a patterned (or a coordinating) fabric for curtains in the bedroom and blinds in the bathroom; echo the colour of the bathroom wall tiles in the bedroom wall treatment, perhaps using matching borders in both areas; and pick accessories which also relate to both schemes.

The Bedroom

Bedrooms are usually highly personal spaces. In addition to being used for sleeping, changing clothes, etc., and as a private area in which to relax

away from the rest of the family, they provide storage space for personal possessions. In some cases a bedroom may double as a study, workroom or playroom – as well as being somewhere to sleep.

Most bedrooms can be coloured, styled, decorated and furnished in a more individual way than the communal areas of the home, although shared spaces (master bedroom, childrens' rooms) need very careful furnishing and styling to satisfy all the occupants.

The first essential item is a comfortable bed, which can be

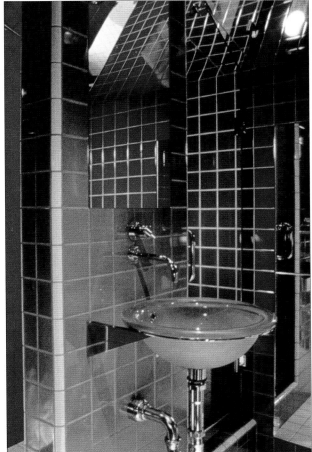

◄ Two tones of glazed plain wall tiles are hung trellis-fashion to create a dado, bordered with a plain contrasting tile. Coordinating larger floor pavers echo the diamond design on the wall.

▼ Plain tiles in contrasting rich, dark and pale, cool colours, grouted in white for greater emphasis, create a sophisticated, individual scheme very simply.

◄◄ This bathroom is completely tiled and floored to coordinate with the elegant fittings. Bathroom floor tiles must always be non-slip.

selected to fit in with your chosen theme – from an opulently draped four-poster or Victorian brass bedstead, to streamlined sofa bed or futon. The choice of bed also depends on the style of the room. If you want it to stand out and dominate, dress it extravagantly to contrast with the floor and wall treatments, although these could link up with the other fabrics in the scheme. If you want it to be self-effacing, cover the bed to blend in with the surroundings (floor and walls).

Adequate storage is the next thing to consider. Whenever possible, plan this from the inside out, figuring out exactly what you need to store, and designing cupboards and units around personal requirements. For free-standing furniture, check interior as well as exterior measurements to make sure it will hold all the things you need to put in it. Check the depth and bases of drawers, as well as ease of opening and the strength of runners to be sure they will not collapse. For a more traditional theme, a Victorian or Edwardian washstand with a tiled or marble top can hold the conventional "jug-and-basin" set, or be used as a practical dressing table surface, or even be adapted to take a plumbed-in basin. Old wooden-topped dressing tables and washstands can be tiled with a suitable ceramic tile, although the framework may need strengthening to take the extra weight. Use the type of grout manufactured for use in the kitchen to be impervious to spillages. This piece could be coordinated into the scheme with a matching tiled splashback.

Room to Relax

Choose the colour scheme and pattern "mix" with relaxation in mind. Avoid strongly contrasting colours and bold patterns unless the room is very light and airy, or you want to set a stimulating scheme for a child. Too many shiny textures,

◄ Large strong-coloured tiles with a diamond border show off the all-white fixtures to great effect.

▼ Gleaming white wall tiles have an inset border to outline the bathtub and other features. Coordinating floor tiles draw the eye to the attractive older style, cast-iron tub.

► An all-white bathroom relies on contrast of curving forms and neat geometric tiling for effect. Colour accents can be changed to suit the mood – or the season.

especially on walls, can be dazzling, so incorporate delicate light-filtering fabrics, slatted blinds and shutters, lace-trimmed bedlinens and wicker items for a feminine feel and to provide textural contrast.

The lighter values of the cooler colours (lilac, silvers, soft greens, pale blues) will help to create a peaceful mood and will add an impression of light and space. These colours may be too unwelcoming in a cold, dark room, so use soft yellows or warm peach with gold or terracotta, and contrast with sparkling white or subtle creams, accented with sharp blues or glossy greens. Alternatively, use frankly feminine pinks, teamed with sophisticated rose, "cooled" with navy blue, lavender or grey. If these softer shades or sugar-sweet florals are too pretty for a shared

bedroom, look at the sophisticated "true" neutrals – different tones of grey with black and white, and enliven the scheme with a few bright accents. Or perhaps the more "earthy" neutrals might be more appropriate – warm browns and burnt-orange, teamed with burlap (hessian)-beige, taupe, ecru, creams, and spiced up with Chinese jade and aqua greens, or lapis-lazuli blues.

Childrens' bedrooms require different considerations. There is plenty of scope for imaginative treatments – colours can be bold, stimulating primaries, or use the slightly softer sugared-almond colours. There are many specialist designs available on wallcoverings, borders, tiles, bedding, fabrics and accessories, but you can create your own scene with murals, stencils,

posters, etc. Remember that children soon tire of current fads and outgrow nursery, film or television characters even more quickly than they do child-sized furniture!

Teenagers' rooms can be more sophisticated, with subtle middle-tone shades chosen to suit the owner and their particular interests – for instance, "racing" green teamed with terracotta; the favourite football team's colours; black, deep blue with grey and white, decorated with silver stars; the more feminine pinks, lilacs and mauves associated with ballet, etc. Whatever scheme you select for such rooms, choose practical, washable surfaces for floors and walls.

A Different Dimension
Most bedrooms have plenty of richly textured curtains and soft furnishings

which create a gentle, welcoming mood. These can be emphasized and contrasted with tiled and other hard flooring, particularly in a dual-purpose bedroom and playroom. Rugs (non-slip) can provide under-foot comfort on cooler days, especially if the theme is minimalist, country style, colourful Mediterranean, or eclectic ethnic. They are also good to use where children indulge in messy play.

Ceramic tiles can also be used for splashbacks on walls behind any basin or dressing table, and make a really practical surface treatment in a baby-changing area. The harsh texture of the basin and tiles can be offset with a frilled or pleated fabric valance, perhaps in fabric to match the window treatment, and attached to hide the pipework or table legs.

◄ A raised four-tile fish panel in soft colours provides an attractive focus above the faucet.

▲ Alphabet tiles, set here as a decorative panel above a baby-changing area, can be used as a border or insets in almost any room.

► Blue and white floral tiles above a bedroom sink area frame the mirrors, linking them with the walls and counters to create a sparkling effect.

COLOUR
DIRECTORY

USING COLOUR AND PATTERN – THE BASICS

When designing, refurbishing, decorating or furnishing any room, there are certain basic principles to consider; and four allies to help you achieve stunning results – colour, pattern, texture and form.

Colour helps to create a mood or ambience, and can suggest a specific traditional flavour. Colours can be combined for a stimulating or a relaxing effect. They can be used to warm up cold areas and to cool down hot ones. Colour can create space visually and introduce a feeling of cosy intimacy.

Patterns can set the style of a room, as well as provide visual interest. Certain designs used on major surfaces will set a modern or authentic period look. Pattern, like colour, can be used to help adjust the visual proportions of a room. They can both be used to emphasize good features and play down ugly ones.

Texture exists on every surface – some are shiny and light-reflecting, and others are matt, flat and light-absorbing. Sculpted, rough and rustic textures rely on the play of light across their surface for maximum effect, while light-filtering ones diffuse the light. Textures in turn relate to the colour on the surface – making it brighter (light-reflecting), darker or duller (light-absorbing), or more fragile and delicate (light-filtering). Contrast in texture is essential to a successful scheme.

Form, or shape, is another important "ingredient." It can be square or oblong and angular, linear, softly flowing, or rounded and curvaceous. Aim for a balance of forms in a room, combining several different shapes on both the horizontal and vertical planes.

Colour Theory

There are three basic types of colour – warm, cool and neutral.

Warm advancing colours can warm up a space or create a cosy feel in a large room. Because they appear to come forwards, they can be enclosing, especially in their brighter versions. Examples are red-violet, red, red-orange, orange, yellow-orange, yellow, some yellow-greens, and all their different values (strength or weight of colour) from palest pink, lemon, peach and apricot to deep wine reds, glowing golds and earthy terracottas.

Cool receding colours in their palest values create an impression of cool elegance and space as they seem to go away from you. They can be used to cool down a hot or very sunny room. However, brighter versions of cool colours can be demanding. Examples are violets, blue-violets, blue, blue-green, greens and some yellow-greens – and their different tints, tones and shades, from palest lavender and misty sky blues to deepest forest and olive greens. On the colour wheel, the warm (advancing) colours are on one side, and on the other are the cool (receding) ones.

Neutrals are the colours which do not appear on the colour wheel. They are used to link, contrast, or help to define a colour scheme. Neutrals can be used as a background colour, although they can be very effective on their own, especially where a minimalist or simple relaxing mood is required. The "true" neutrals are black, white and pure grey. Grey is made by mixing white and black together, and depending on the proportions used, can range from pale silver to deep charcoal. There are also "accepted" neutrals – cream, off-white, beige and the colours of natural materials. Many "accepted" neutrals have cool, receding or warm, advancing qualities.

Colour Harmonizing

It is, of course, the way colours are used together that gives a room mood, character and style. There are several accepted ways of colour scheming called "colour harmonies" – although they are not necessarily harmonious! To create a balanced colour scheme, it is essential to have tonal contrast, achieved by introducing different strengths (or values) of colour.

A **complementary colour scheme** uses colours opposite each other on the colour wheel – red and green, orange and blue, lilac and yellow – in all their tonal variations. For example, pale pink and forest green, terracotta and turquoise, mauve and gold are all complementary schemes. As these schemes combine a warm, advancing colour with a cool, receding one, the effect is usually dramatic.

An **adjacent colour scheme** is when "neighbourly" colours (next to each other on the colour wheel) are used together. Several segments – two, three, four or five – can make up the scheme. When the blues and greens are used, the effect is cool; warm adjacent neighbours (yellow, gold and burnt-orange) create a cosy feel. Either "mix" is more relaxing than a complementary scheme. A combination of cool and warm colours next to each other is more stimulating – for example, blue, green, yellow-greens, yellow or orange with magenta, lilac, blue and blue-green.

A **monochromatic colour scheme** (sometimes called a tone-on-tone scheme) uses different values (strengths) of one colour. It is essential to use different tones of colour to avoid a bland and boring scheme. It also helps to contrast such schemes with a suitable neutral and to introduce a strong accent colour in accessories, taken from the opposite side of the colour wheel. When choosing glazed ceramic tiles, remember that the colour will often look much brighter or stronger *en masse* due to the light reflecting off the surface. Patterns can be surprisingly deceptive, especially if you have only seen a single tile.

Picking Patterns

As with warm and cool colours, patterns can be advancing or receding. Bold geometric, floral and regular repeating designs tend to advance and so look stronger when spread over a large floor, wall or window area. Such bold effects are best used in big rooms where they can be fully appreciated. Small patterns work like receding colours, having a tendency to fade into insignificance when spread over a large surface. They are best used in smaller rooms or where a feeling of space is required. It is essential to relate the strength of the colour and the boldness of the pattern to the size of the surface – they should always be in the correct scale.

In most supplier's and manufacturer's collections you will find a wide range of colours, patterns, styles and textures. One exciting way to use colourful tiles is to create a patch-work pattern – but make sure that the tiles are of the same depth and strength.

It can be difficult to relate a small sample or only one tile to the finished effect on a whole wall or floor. Illustrations in leaflets, pattern books or on packaging can give an impression of how the design works, but never put your trust in them for colour-matching. Always try to see as large a sample as possible of any fabrics, wallcovering or paint, etc., and on the correct plane. Gather fabric for curtains/shades in your hand to get a more accurate idea of how it will look when made.

Group several tiles together (especially if they are patterned) so you can see how the design "travels" across the surface. Some suppliers display wall tiles mounted on pull-out boards and floor tiles in drawers, or in special mirrored boxes so you can judge the effect more easily. If you are not offered any of these displays, you may have to open a box and set out some of the tiles on a flat surface.

Colour and patterns for tiles, bathroom fixtures, kitchen units and work surfaces need to be very carefully considered since they are all semi-permanent fixtures and will probably have several schemes worked around them during their lifetime, so try to plan ahead. This is equally true of the floor. All the tiles and slabs in this book are classed as hard floorings and become a permanent part of the structure of a room once they are installed. So again, when deciding on design and choosing colour, think about the need to plan future colour schemes.

Professional interior designers plan a scheme from the floor up, unless there is already an existing limitation in the room. Almost everything in the room is seen in relation to it – walls and woodwork (baseboard [skirting], doors) butt up to it; drapes and curtains touch it; furniture, appliances and equipment "sit" on it. So bear all these things in mind when choosing flooring.

Finally, never underestimate the importance of colour "sampling." Always obtain adequately sized samples of any proposed materials (at least one tile, preferably several) and look at them in the room where you propose to use them under *exact lighting conditions* – both in daylight and night (artificial) light.

ROSY
REDS

RICH REDS AND PURPLES ARE VIBRANT AND EXCITING. THEY
ARE THE STRONGEST OF THE ADVANCING COLOURS AND
CAN BE USED TO DECREASE THE SIZE OF A ROOM
VISUALLY AND MAKE IT SEEM MORE WELCOMING
AND COSY. PALER PINKS AND VIOLETS
ARE SHADES OF SENSUALITY,
WELL-BEING AND ENCHANTMENT.
RED'S COMPLEMENTARY
COLOUR IS GREEN;
PURPLE'S IS
YELLOW.

RED
TILE
DIRECTORY

Red is the most attention-grabbing colour in the spectrum. It is the strongest of the hot advancing colours. It is associated with energy, vitality, happiness, richness and luxury, but also with aggressiveness and danger. But red is also a romantic colour – a gift of red roses is a traditional love token. Its paler value, pink, suggests tenderness, affection and femininity, as well as good health, high spirits and optimism.

Purple, violet and mauve are all found between red and blue on the colour wheel, where the warm and cool colours meet. Purple can therefore be warm or cool. These colours represent sensitivity, knowledge, sanctity, humility, nostalgia and sorrow. Strong purple radiates self-esteem and confidence. Violet is the colour of Mary Magdalene and the god Jupiter. The paler mauves and violets are shades of sensuality and enchantment, and are linked with good taste and an appreciation of the arts, music, philosophy and ballet.

Bold reds appear to come towards you and can be used to make a space look smaller, warmer and more welcoming. A cold bathroom with clinical-looking white equipment and tiles can be made much more user-friendly with a subtle pink and rose red colour scheme. However, if the brighter values of red are used indiscriminately, they can induce a claustrophobic and over-stimulating sensation. A scheme incorporating

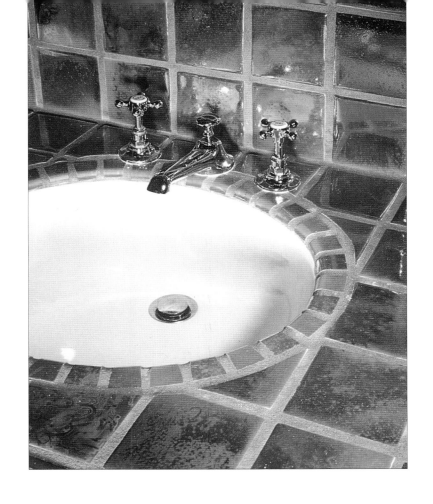

strong values of red and green (the complementary of red) will be very stimulating and best used in areas where you want to discourage lingering, such as a family bathroom or a cold, bleak hall.

Like red, purple in its strongest value is vibrant and demanding, and can therefore be overpowering, so it needs to be contrasted with pastel colours or subtle neutrals. A tone-on-tone scheme of purples and violets with white, black and grey will set a modern, sophisticated scene in a formal room – especially one with a Gothic flavour, where the black accents can be provided in wrought-iron fixtures. The slightly grey or plum tones of reddish-purple are

warm and inviting, and look very elegant in the right setting – for instance, an imposing hall, a formal dining room or an opulent bedroom, especially in an older-style property.

Lilac has long been a forgotten colour but is coming back into its own, particularly in the bathroom. It is also a surprisingly effective, but rarely used, colour for a kitchen – lilac wall tiles and a deeper grey-purple on the floor can be the perfect foil for dark spruce green units, or Shaker green free-standing kitchen furniture.

The adjacent colours to purple are blue on one side of the colour wheel and red on the other. Blue-purples and violets are wonderfully refreshing when teamed with blues and greens – a good combination for a warm kitchen or sunny conservatory. When mixed with the warmer neighbours (reds and pinks), the effect can be very cosy.

Mexican handmade, hand-decorated glazed tiles
These tiles are shaped to fit around a hand basin which has been decorated to match with a stylized floral motif.

Brazilian glazed ceramic wall tiles
The deep red field tiles look wonderful with this mosaic-style border. The different shades of blue, together with the bright white grout, have a cooling effect.

French handmade glazed wall tiles
These bright pink tiles are topped with a traditional raised leaf border in white and framed underneath with a solid red liner. The central diamonds are in white and red, demonstrating the different effects which can be achieved quite easily with such a simple change of colour.

Moroccan handmade floor tiles
These are made from stone, marble and white cement mix using the traditional encaustic method. The pattern is created by using plain tiles laid diamond-fashion, finished with surrounding borders to create the look of a decorative rug.

"Red" tiles range from palest pink, through dusky rose to crimson and scarlet. When floral designs are used with this colour, the effect is simply stunning.

Italian glazed wall tiles
These frostproof tiles have jewel-bright motifs framed within a red background and scatter patterns of red, white, black and blue. Experiment by teaming them with solid white or black tiles to produce starkly different effects.

Italian matt-glazed wall tiles
A subtle horizontal effect is created by combining pink, red and white – an effective treatment to widen a narrow wall area visually with plain tiles.

Italian glazed wall tiles
Modern abstract patterns used as a whole tile or as a border to a solid white centre create a bright and cheerful effect. The two dominant colours in the designs are red and yellow, so coordinate with plain tiles in these colours to create unusual effects.

Italian glazed wall tiles
The solid colours and random stripe create a stylish treatment. Use this type of tile design only on level, perfectly square walls or they could appear to be slipping off!

Spanish glazed wall tiles
The octagonal-shaped white tiles have bright red square insets dropped in diamond-fashion at the corners and are outlined with a narrow red-and-white diamond pattern and white raised rope border to form a stylish splashback or border.

Hand-glazed wall tiles

These deep pinkish-purple tones would look good with matching and coordinating hand basins and patterned tiles.

French glazed wall tiles

Abstract-patterned drop-in tiles are teamed with candy-coloured purple and green plain tiles. They are ideal for a child's room or a family bathroom.

Porcelain glazed tiles and liners

These tiles create an attractive textured geometric effect ideal for bathrooms and shower rooms.

Italian textured earthenware tiles

In wonderful jewel-rich colours and ethnic patterns, these tiles can be combined to create panels, frames, etc. The seashore theme makes them ideal for a bathroom but they would need sealing with a penetrating sealer, preferably before hanging, as they would not be waterproof in a shower situation.

Glazed ceramic wall tiles

These tiles are hand-coloured to produce variegated shades of pink. The deeper pink and white liner acts as a link with the pastel blue border.

American handmade, hand-moulded, thickly-glazed wall tiles

Use these for bathroom, kitchen and utility areas with coordinating borders, relief nosings and other shapes. The rich colours go right through the spectrum from pale pink to deep bluish-purple and would warm up the coldest bathroom.

There are many beautiful shades of pink and purple which will provide a delicate warmth to a room, particularly when teamed with a textured material or a paint effect such as stippling.

French glazed ceramic wall tiles

Gingham checks and mini-geometrics in clear pink are hand-painted on a white ground. These tiles can be used to create a patchwork pattern, and/or mixed with plain pink or white field tiles.

Glazed ceramic wall tiles

Different modules can be used to build up a wall panel. The central row of square tiles are bordered by quarter-size white tiles and then a floral border. The different-sized tiles add extra visual interest. Although the central row of tiles is primarily blue, the softest hint of graduated red tones are added to introduce a subtle but effective warmth to the design.

Hand-painted glazed wall tiles

This bunch of luscious aubergines look as though they are hanging from a pine strip. Make a decorative panel with three of them or use them as single features.

Italian textured earthenware tiles

The rich shades of purple are combined with ethnic patterns to create a stunning panel. The desert theme of the tiles makes them ideal for a conservatory or bathroom.

Glazed ceramic and terracotta tiles

Dramatic effect is created with a combination of different-sized tiles in subtle Arts & Crafts glazes. They can be used on floors (light use), countertops, for fireplaces and stoves, as wall panels and dados. The reddish glaze is stronger on the outer border, thus drawing more attention to the lighter central area.

Brazilian hand-painted glazed wall tiles

A 50s abstract pattern is used as a border to enclose a panel of plain-coloured tiles with a bold purple contrasting square.

French ceramic wall tiles

Pastel pink and grey-green tiles look attractive in bathrooms. The ridged diamond patterns on the liners have a handcrafted look, further emphasized by the thick white grout and the combination of tile shapes.

Machine-made glazed wall and fireplace tiles

This authentic Art Deco design is based on established patterns of the period. Soft pinks and lilacs are combined with black and grey for a sophisticated scheme. The different tiles can be used to build up a panel; form fireplace columns; outline a feature; make a decorative dado rail – ideal in an Edwardian hall.

Muted shades of pink bear a strong affinity to terracotta and have the same warmth. They are beautiful as plain tiles laid in geometric designs or teamed with floral patterns.

Spanish handmade terracotta tiles
Suitable for floors and walls, these plain tiles are surrounded by a stunning mosaic border made up of a spectrum of colours. The tiles are porous and therefore need sealing.

Italian glazed wall and floor tiles
These stylish minimalist stripes in clear red on white can be combined with a coordinating horizontal striped border when used on walls.

Glazed ceramic tiles
The upper row of pink and white triangles would look good as drop-ins amongst turquoise tiles; the lower row would form an attractive border on a plain wall area.

Handcrafted, rustic moulded tiles
This fan frieze with ram's head insets has a Gothic flavour and makes a perfect border for a fireplace. It could also be used on walls and exterior facades.

Italian glazed wall tiles
These tiles have blocked and striped colour geometric effects in monochromatic tones on white. Mix and match them to create decorative and unusual patterned effects with what are virtually plain tiles.

Italian glazed wall tiles
The slanting abstract pattern in soft pink links with the neat deeper pink edging on the border tile, ideal for bathroom walls.

Hand-decorated glazed wall tiles

The floral patterns are combined with plain coordinating red colour-wash tiles to create a chequerboard-effect wall panel.

Antiqued relief-patterned glazed tiles

The grapes and vine leaves are in warm earth colours and frame a panel of coordinating field tiles. They can be used to form borders, panels, patterns or as drop-ins on walls, or around stoves and fireplaces.

Glazed ceramic wall tiles

From deep crimson to peony pink, red-toned tiles make the perfect surround for a fireplace, enhancing the warmth of the room. These field tiles, liners and floral-patterned drop-ins have a traditional appeal.

Spanish glazed clay tiles

The red floral border has a purple stripe around it to help distinguish the liners from the central panel of tiles. A coloured grout would have the same effect.

Hand-painted matt-glazed tiles

These tiles build up to form a daisy mural of colourful flowers which spring from a coordinating jug. The softly flowing leaf border echos the leaves in the bouquet. The panel would be an eye-catching focal point in a plain tiled wall, or pretty as a splashback in a windowless area.

"Picture" tiles are widely available to use as drop-ins on walls and countertops. They are a simple and effective method of enlivening a plain area.

Glazed ceramic wall tiles
This picture panel has been treated to produce a handcrafted look. The autumnal fruits and leaves with blackbird border make this ideal for a kitchen, particularly one without a view.

American glazed wall tiles
These tiles are decorated to depict a basket of luscious strawberries, ideal for kitchens or appropriate commercial situations.

Screen-printed glazed wall tiles
These have a flowing floral design in pinks and greens on a soft white ground. Twelve tiles form a panel with the bolder bouquet spreading across the central tiles.

Hand-decorated heatproof glazed tiles
These Victorian-style tiles can be used to form panels, borders, dados, etc., but can also be used as insets for fireplaces to create a traditional look.

Hand-decorated glazed wall tiles
This tiled panel is suitable for bathrooms, showers, kitchens or fireplaces. It could be used effectively above a sink, bath or stove, or as an interesting feature on a blank wall. The border tiles can be used to top a splashback or create a dado rail.

VIBRANT
ORANGES

ORANGE IS ONE OF THE WARMEST COLOURS. THE BOLD
VALUES ARE ALMOST AS INTENSE AND AS ADVANCING
AS RED, AND IN NATURE THEY ARE TEMPERED
WITH COOL COLOURS. THE PALER, MORE
SUBTLE ORANGE TINTS AND TONES
ARE WARM AND WELCOMING,
AND ACT AS A "SUNSHINE"
COLOUR. ITS
COMPLEMENTARY
COLOUR IS
BLUE.

ORANGE

TILE DIRECTORY

Orange is one of the warmest colours — the bold values are strident, domineering and almost as intense and advancing as red. The paler and more subtle tints and tones — such as peach, apricot, melon and terracotta — are warm and welcoming and, like yellow, act as a "sunshine" colour. Orange is also the colour of the earth; deep orange-brown clays are used to make floor and wall tiles; copper and bronze are both orange with a metallic lustre; and gemstones include topaz, amber and citrine quartz. In nature the colour is found in exotic birds, butterflies and fish; summer flowerbeds are radiant with orange flowers, and autumn is ablaze with the variety of tones in the changing foliage and harvest fruits.

Orange combines the physical energy of red with the intellect of yellow — the two hues mixed together create pure orange. In heraldry orange symbolizes strength and endurance, and in Greek mythology it was associated with Zeus, ruler of the gods. In Buddhism orange suggests humility — hence the saffron robes (it was also the dress colour for the humble in earlier times; for example, clerks wore orange-tawny). To the Chinese and Japanese, it is the colour of love and happiness. In Europe orange is a colour of temptation: paintings depict Eve seducing Adam with an orange or a peach instead of an apple. Auburn hair is also synonymous with the temptress — the romantic heroines of Pre-Raphaelite paintings have long, thick, auburn hair, and in Ancient Rome women hennaed their hair to please their husbands. Bold orange is very stimulating, so it is wise to confine strong tones to the smaller surfaces in a room, or use it for accents or as part of an overall patterned surface. When orange is teamed with its complementary colour blue, or combined with black or grey and white, it is best used for rooms not intended for relaxation – for example, playrooms.

In nature, the more fiery oranges are nearly always tempered with cool green foliage, set against a clear blue or misty grey sky, or perhaps seen in relation to rich earthy browns or natural stone and wood. These are all good colour combinations to bring indoors to create an elegant atmosphere of warmth and welcome. Subtle shades of burnt-orange or chestnut teamed with creamy beige and bright blue are the traditional colours of Victorian encaustic tiled floors. With this colour range shifted up a gear to strong orange, Madonna blue, jade and ochre with crisp white, a Mediterranean ambience is suggested.

The bolder and darker values of orange also need some neutral touches, as well as colour contrasts, to use them to full advantage. Black, white and grey work well with the terracotta tones – an "Etruscan" combination very popular in the seventeenth and eighteenth centuries and evocative of Josiah Wedgwood's Jasperware. Such colour schemes are elegant and inviting, but can also seem enclosing. The paler tones – e.g., peach or apricot – create a more relaxed, natural theme and may also need neutral touches and balancing with rich chestnut or dark, warm browns.

Mexican handmade, hand-painted glazed wall tiles

Use these to drop in as insets, or to form a feature panel.

Hand-decorated glazed wall tiles

Inspired by Islamic decoration and William Morris florals of the Victorian era, here soft terracotta is used with its complement blue. Many permutations and other colour combinations could be used to create different traditional effects.

Glazed ceramic wall tiles

A clean, summery look is achieved with soft apricot and plain white tiles. Here, a patterned border and drop-in tiles are highlighted with touches of blue and yellow.

Portuguese hand-painted glazed ceramic wall tiles

The traditional floral motif forms a geometric pattern when hung as a splashback, panel or dado. The single motif tile could be used as a border to finish a plain tiled area, in a coordinating colour.

French faience-glazed wall tiles

These tiles can be combined with plain field tiles to form a dado effect for bathrooms, kitchens, utility rooms, conservatories, halls, etc. The overall effect of this dahlia design is of a summery flower-filled windowbox.

Plain terracotta tiles are ideal where an earthy, rustic look is required. They are attractive as a backdrop for pictorial drop-ins and borders as well as for use in geometric designs.

Hand-decorated glazed tiles
These tiles depict autumnal-coloured fruit, tumbling out of a rustic basket, ideal for kitchen sink/countertop splashbacks or behind stoves.

Mexican handcut, hand-decorated glazed wall tiles
The central pure white tiles are set diamond-fashion inside the blue-orange border for extra visual interest.

Handmade mosaic border tiles
The scroll, chevron or wave pattern can be set into a terracotta floor to create a decorative design – ideal for floors where the mosaic border can outline features or define the shape of the area.

Hand-decorated clay wall tiles
Plain tiles are interspersed with brightly coloured picture tiles and contrasting turquoise blue liner, ideal for a child's room or bathroom.

Unglazed terracotta floor tiles
These hexagonal tiles are used without insets to form a classic patchwork pattern; they are handmade from Barro clay for a warm surface.

Handmade unglazed terracotta floor tiles
These characteristic burnt-orange tiles can be combined with insets in self-colour to build up a traditional geometric pattern.

Handmade unglazed terracotta floor tiles
In warm burnt orange, square tiles are enclosed by interlocking lozenge-shaped tiles to create a classic geometric design.

Handmade unglazed terracotta floor tiles
Square tiles are laid diamond-fashion and bordered with same-size square tiles to create a traditional geometric effect. Plain tiles can be used in many ways to create a design without actually being patterned.

Handmade reclaimed terracotta floor tiles
These are laid brick fashion, with patterned drop-ins to provide extra colour and pattern interest. Oblong tiles can be used to create herringbone patterns, to form borders or define areas.

Terracotta tiles are extremely popular and are available in a wide range of shapes as they are most commonly used to create geometric or traditional brick patterns for floors.

Italian glazed clay floor tiles
This subtle stencilled/batik look is ideal for kitchen floors and countertops. They would make an ideal border to either a plain or patterned floor.

American inlaid terracotta floor tiles
The traditional geometric pattern in subtle blue complements the characteristic orange. These tiles can be laid chequerboard-fashion with plain terracotta field tiles, or as an elegant border.

Glazed quarry tiles
A patchwork of blue and terracotta tiles is bordered by crosses in a circular design to produce a Gothic look. These tiles are suitable for walls and work surfaces.

Glazed quarry tiles
Suitable for use on walls and countertops, this wonderful Gothic pattern has rich, exciting colour combinations.

Glazed wall tiles
These tiles are combined with chequerboard and star liner tiles and a ridged cornice to form an elegant, traditional dado treatment.

Handmade unglazed terracotta floor tiles
These tiles are set out to form a traditional geometric pattern with deep-coloured liners and bright insets.

Glazed quarry tiles
Deep reds and rustic terracotta are offset with a blue patterned border to produce a distinctive Arts & Crafts flavour. The tiles are suitable for walls or countertops.

SUNSHINE
YELLOWS

YELLOW IS THE COLOUR OF THE SUN'S LIFE-GIVING RAYS.
IT WILL BRING A FEELING OF SUNSHINE, WARMTH
AND LIGHT INTO A COLD, DARK ROOM.
PALER VALUES CREATE A SENSE OF SPACE,
ESPECIALLY IF USED ON SHINY
TEXTURED SURFACES SUCH
AS GLAZED TILES. ITS
COMPLEMENTARY
COLOUR IS VIOLET
OR PURPLE.

YELLOW

TILE DIRECTORY

Yellow is the colour of the sun's life-giving rays and is associated with well-being, intellect and creative energy. Yellow suggests power, wealth, royalty, privilege and pageantry (being the colour of the medieval "field of the cloth of gold") and in heraldry it symbolizes honour and loyalty.

For Christians and Hindus yellow is

the colour of life and truth; in ancient Greece and Rome it represented the arts and learning and was the colour of Athena, goddess of wisdom.

Yellow is also closely associated with nature – it is the warm welcoming colour of spring flowers emerging after winter's gloom, from palest primrose to eye-stopping daffodil. The clear sunshine yellows, sand golds and sunflowers associated with summer and the blue sky can all be contrasted with the rich, glowing golds and bronzes of autumn foliage and harvest.

Yellow is a warm, advancing colour and has a high reflective value. In all its versions – from sharp citron to opulent gold – yellow will bring a feeling of sunshine, warmth and light into any cold, dark room or brighten up an area overshadowed by tall buildings or trees. The paler values create a sense of space, especially if used on shiny textured surfaces such as glazed tiles to maximize reflected light.

Lemon and grapefruit yellows combine well with other mouth-watering citrus colours such as lime, tangerine and persimmon to create a related scheme in a kitchen or bathroom.

Or clear yellows mixed with the sweet-pea and freesia colours of magenta, mauve, lilac and pink, sparked with white, create a romantic mood in a bedroom.

Exciting effects can be made by contrasting warm advancing colours with cool receding ones – for example, the warmth of yellow balanced with glossy leaf greens is a combination often seen in nature; think of daffodils or sunflowers. There are numerous such combinations for different effects, and the warm colour always appears dominant. To achieve a 50/50 balance, use one-third warm yellow to two-thirds cold contrast. Yellow also works well on its own in a tone-on-tone colour scheme as long as there is plenty of tonal and textural contrast.

The complementary colour of yellow is lilac, violet or purple, and when used together this combination can be visually very stimulating. The tones should therefore be varied to create a more subtle effect – for instance, pale primrose yellow with bluish-purples and deep gold and touches of brass with lavender.

In a large unwelcoming hall, daunting drawing room or big baronial building, yellow can be mixed with other warm, advancing colours to create an atmosphere of cosy intimacy. When used with deep terracotta, Indian red, wine and strong fuchsia pinks – or even scarlet – yellow will provide the light relief to a bold, exciting scheme. Such rich combinations need off-setting with a neutral colour, or when mixed with black and burnished mahogany brown, it creates a sophisticated Regency, Empire or Egyptian theme.

Hand-decorated glazed wall tile
This tile looks like a traditional Delft-style panel. It is edged with a narrow slip border and corner insets in the background colour, with contrasting brush line detail, to work as a drop-in or feature tile.

Hand-decorated glazed wall tiles
A 12-tile panel of floral motif tiles is built up to suggest a spring field full of bright yellow daffodils; the border tiles could be used to top a splashback panel of plain tiles.

Handmade, hand-painted glazed wall tiles
Combined with an off-white plain field tile, these tiles build up to form a decorative bright yellow and green daffodil pattern which looks like a springtime window box. Use this type of tile design to create panels, splashbacks or as an important feature in a dark, cold, sunless room. Glazed ceramic tiles are light-reflecting, and yellow is a particularly good colour to use to create a feeling of space and light.

Glazed wall tiles
The central nine-tile panel forms a country-style pitcher filled with yellow flowers. Here it is combined with six culinary border tiles.

Fruits and flowers in sunny shades of yellow are ideal for both homes and commercial situations such as a restaurant, fruit or health food store.

Italian handmade Majolica-glazed terracotta wall tiles

These classic rustic tiles have a lemon-tree border design with matching corner tiles in sharp lemon and green on a white crackle-glaze ground.

Hand-painted glazed mural wall panel

This six-piece panel creates an authentic botanical look, reminiscent of old prints. It can be used to form a panel or as a frieze. The strong ochre and rose are combined with silvery-green leaves on a cream background.

Portuguese glazed wall and fireplace tiles

These charmingly rustic tiles can also be used on countertops and floors (light use), creating flowing floral patterns.

Portuguese glazed wall and fireplace tiles

These tiles would make a sophisticated border to form a neat finish to wall panels, dados or to frame salient features.

Spanish glazed clay tiles

Ripe fruits form a decorative border around four crackle-glazed tiles which have been treated with a peach colourwash.

Hand-crafted clay wall tiles

This blue-and-yellow floral splashback panel is given added textural interest by the use of raised grouting.

Italian glazed tiles

This four-tile traditional panel has a strong Mediterranean flavour, suggesting sunshine and warm summer days. The swirling formal pattern will repeat from tile to tile to create a geometric effect.

Italian glazed ceramic wall tiles
Solid yellow tiles are laid brick-fashion and enhanced with blue border stripes.

Mexican handmade glazed ceramic wall tiles
Clear bright colours such as this sunny yellow would cheer up a cold kitchen or bathroom. These tiles can be combined with coordinating patterned ones.

American geometric-patterned quarry tiles
In sunshine colours with *cuerda seca*-style glaze, these tiles can be used as borders, insets and drop-ins to add interest to a plain quarry-tiled floor.

Italian glazed wall tiles
A narrow raised relief diamond border acts as a focus between the square and linear tiles on either side.

Italian glazed wall tiles
In bright, slightly mottled glaze, these yellow tiles are set diamond-fashion and combined with white diamonds and triangles to form a border with a moulded nosing in deep green and blue.

Glazed wall tiles
These Art Nouveau patterned border tiles in yellow and white form a panel with contrasting geometrics and are echoed in a contrasting pink border.

Hand-decorated glazed wall tiles
The all-over repeating pattern of fruit and leaves is reminiscent of Arts & Crafts flowing floral design. Here, nine tiles are used to form a splashback panel.

Bold, cheerful designs – elephants, circus clowns, flowers and abstract shapes – are a trademark of these yellow tiles, making them particularly useful for a child's room.

English hand-crafted glazed ceramic wall tiles
These tiles are patterned with yellow frogs on a white ground. Here, two tiles form a panel to show the frog leaping across the seam; however, other amusing leapfrog sequences could be planned. It could be combined with a barleytwist border in coordinating yellow, or contrasting green or dark blue.

Handmade, hand-decorated wall panel
These hand-painted glazed tiles have a harvest theme, with glossy wheatsheaf relief; they are ideal for warming up a cold kitchen or for use in a bakery or restaurant.

Spanish handmade terracotta wall tiles
These traditional tiles are glazed in white and hand-decorated with cheerful food and kitchen motifs that can be built up to form an interesting splashback or mural. Here, the design incorporates wine, fruit and fish, ideal for a kitchen or dining room.

Hand-painted wall mural
This mural features sunny yellow, cream, strong blue and soft sage greens to make building up a coordinating colour scheme easier.

REFRESHING
GREENS

GREEN IS THE COLOUR OF NATURE AND SUGGESTS
GROWTH AND REGENERATION. IT IS THE COLOUR OF
THE ENVIRONMENTAL MOVEMENT. MOST GREENS
ARE RECEDING AND RESTFUL; THEY CAN
CREATE AN IMPRESSION OF SPACE AND
INTRODUCE A VERDANT FEEL TO
A SUNLESS APARTMENT OR
DRAB BASEMENT. ITS
COMPLEMENTARY
COLOUR IS
RED.

GREEN
TILE
DIRECTORY

green is the true colour of nature. It is synonymous with foliage, flora, fields and forests, and it suggests growth and regeneration — it is the colour of new leaves. Green is always refreshing to look at — a verdant view is excellent relief for tired eyes. In heraldry green is the symbol of hope and growth. It is the sacred colour of Islam, and in the Christian church green vestments symbolize the Resurrection and eternal life. The Greeks associated it with Venus, the goddess of love and fertility, and her sacred plant, the evergreen myrtle. The current Green movement strives for the protection of the environment and stands against pollution.

Green is a balancing colour; it lies halfway between the warm and cool sections of the colour wheel. It can be dark, mysterious, sometimes dangerous (jungle greens); jewel-bright and stimulating (aquamarine, emerald or peridot); cool and elegant as it goes toward its cooler neighbour, blue in the colour wheel; and warm and inviting when it is tinged with yellow. Most greens are receding and restful. The paler values can be used to create a calm ambience and an impression of space, and introduce a verdant feel to a sunless city apartment, low-ceilinged attic or drab basement.

Green can be used as an elegant visual link between a garden and a living room, dining room or conservatory. A cool green is a good choice for a kitchen, which is often a hot, steamy centre of activity. Forget the old adage "blue and green should never be seen," as a cool, spacious look can

be created using this combination. If strong values of green and red (green is the complementary of red) are used together, the effect can become uncomfortable. More subtle tones of these colours will create a softer effect.

An all-green tone-on-tone scheme appears subtle and spacious but cool and elegant. The palest version could be used on the ceiling, a deeper shade for the walls, a middle tone for the floor, and the deepest value for furniture and perhaps the paintwork. Use a neutral colour to link them all and then introduce some warm accessories and accent items. The tonal value and strength of the greens determine the depth of the accent colour and should relate to the style of the room.

Combine greens with creamy beige neutrals, natural woods, jute, seagrass and rush matting in a conservatory, country-style kitchen or dining room, cottage bedroom or sitting area – and reintroduce green in foliage plants. Green has always been associated with traditional interiors, particularly those of the Victorian and Edwardian era, when virulent green painted or tiled dados were fashionable. A rich dark green with subtle red can be used to set a Victorian Scottish baronial theme in a large entrance hall, drawing room or study/library. A bold Gothic effect can be created by using "Pugin green" (a clear emerald) with burnt-orange, bold cerulean blue and a touch of purple, all offset with black – introduced in the form of wrought-iron light fixtures, curtain poles and finials, and other accessories.

French handmade, hand-painted glazed wall and countertop tiles
This rich "antique" green creates the characteristic rustic look of Normandy in France.

Italian hand-painted glazed wall tiles
Each individual tile has tonal variations, to create a rustic look.

French hand-glazed terracotta wall tiles
The slight colour variation is caused by the solid glaze. These tiles can be used on bathroom/bedroom countertops and would look good with a coordinating basin.

Mexican handmade terracotta tiles
The solid glaze gives the characteristic dappled look of hand-crafted tiles. These tiles are mainly suitable for walls, although they can be used as colourful drop-ins or key squares in a terracotta tiled floor.

Hand-finished Venetian marble tiles
These can be used on floors and walls for an elegant effect. Take care with marble in a "wet" situation as it can be slippery underfoot.

Mexican hand-painted glazed wall tiles
Coordinating border tiles and mural panels can be used with these subtly coloured tiles to form interesting visual effects.

French hand-glazed terracotta wall tiles
These deep sea green-coloured tiles would look superbly refreshing in a bathroom, particularly as a splashback.

Mexican handmade glazed wall tiles
Combining the patterned bird and scattered flower motif with richly glazed plain tiles in glorious greens shows how easy tile coordination is.

Geometric patterns appear very bold in this range of strong green tiles, whether the pattern is printed onto the tile or the tiles are cut into intricate shapes to form the design.

American glazed wall tiles
These octagonal-shaped tiles are combined with insets and bordered with top-cap moulding in rich green.

Machine-made vitrified wall tiles
Use these tiles to create a monochromatic scheme in tones of pale aquas through to deep green. The exciting colours allow many innovative design possibilities including cut-tile mural design.

Quarried slate with terracotta insets
These tiles are laid to form a classic key-square effect with a slate border. Use them for floors both indoors and out, but bear in mind that calibrated slate needs sealing.

Riven slate floor tiles
These tiles are set in classical fashion with small corner insets and neat narrow borders. They could be laid across a hall, conservatory, kitchen or living-room floor to create the look of traditional flagstones.

Italian glazed terracotta wall tiles
Pale green tiles border a pink diamond with a coordinating pink-and-white nosing to form a pretty bathroom splashback.

Glazed ceramic wall tiles
This geometric diamond pattern is created with different tones of blue-green which could be used as an interesting dado rail-type border on a wall of white tiles.

Natural quarried slate
Warm green slate is laid in a classic brick pattern. Natural slate is multi-coloured and both sides can be used face-up, giving more opportunities for achieving the tonal balance you require.

Riven slate floor tiles
Laid edge-to-edge in brick pattern, the characteristic colour variations and slight veining found in natural quarried products is made into a design feature.

Moroccan quarry floor tiles
Four tiles form a medallion design in rich greens and blues on a cream ground. They would look good teamed with a geometric-patterned border.

Portuguese hand-painted wall tiles
Four tiles are used to form a decorative geometric motif, reminiscent of an heraldic design. They can be repeated across an entire wall area, or used to form drop-in panels.

Hand-decorated glazed wall tiles
This panel of patterned tiles could be set into a border of plain green tiles and grouted in white. Alternatively, use them to form a border around plain tiles for a less busy look.

Glazed wall and floor tiles
These tiles have a matt glaze and can be used to make up a mosaic panel. The blue and light green central tiles are offset by an attractive muted olive surround.

Moroccan handmade encaustic floor tiles
These are made from powdered stone, marble and cement, then cured and dried. Tan and pale ochre plain tiles can be set inside this decorative double border to suggest a Moroccan hand-crafted rug.

Moroccan handmade encaustic floor tiles
Green and ochre field tiles are set diamond-fashion inside a vine-leaf trail border. A simple outer border of ochre tiles finishes the effect.

The green colour of nature lends itself to "natural" designs. All of these are based on leaves and flowers but are given a geometric flavour in their execution.

Mexican glazed wall tiles
Floral and plain tiles in various shades of green are shown. Experiment in this way to decide which colour in the floral design to emphasize with coordinating field tiles.

Mexican hand-painted glazed wall tiles
The bright geometric patterns in two colours on a warm cream ground form a bold design. The tile surface is characteristically uneven.

Glazed ceramic wall tiles
This selection of tiles features glossy relief patterns and intricate geometric and botanical pictorial features. They would be ideal for a conservatory or around a large, Victorian-style fireplace.

Portuguese hand-painted glazed wall tiles
This four-tile panel builds up to create a classic geometric Gothic pattern. It can be set into a plain wall area, or used to build up a stunning overall effect.

Glazed wall tiles
These tiles have a beautiful flowing design and a border stripe. They are suitable as a border to plain tiles on splashbacks and are particularly good for fireplaces.

Hand-decorated wall panel
This panel is built up using oblong tiles, their length helping to accentuate the distance in the country scene. They can be framed with border tiles, a plain frieze, or a moulded border. The panel would be suitable for a bakery or a kitchen without a view.

American hand-painted glazed wall tiles
These tiles are used to build up an Oriental theme to create an unusual and exotic panel. Ideal for Oriental-themed dining rooms, bathrooms or even a restaurant.

Hand-painted, hand-glazed wall tiles
This nine-tile panel creates a country scene. One panel could be used in a small kitchen but four would "balance" a larger room. They are suitable for splashbacks behind burners (hobs) and ranges or perhaps above a sink on a windowless wall.

Welsh glazed wall tiles
A narrow mosaic painted border is used to frame the picture of the fruit tree design to produce a beautiful mural.

Hand-painted glazed wall tiles
The hand-dragged border and harlequin tile pattern in greens and blues is combined with a fruit and fruit bowl motif to add visual interest to wall areas.

The emphasis here is on the fruits of nature – fruits, berries, plants, fish and waterfowl all look wonderful when the colour green is used as the central design theme.

American hand-crafted clay wall tiles

These textured glazed tiles depict a dragonfly, spider and web, butterfly, gecko, salamander and frog on sea greens and blue bases. They could be used as borders and drop-ins to create panels.

American hand-painted glazed wall tiles

The luscious fruits and vegetables have rich green leaves and green glaze outline. They can be used as border tiles, drop-ins or to create exciting wall panels – ideal in a restaurant or speciality food store!

Handmade, hand-painted crackle-glazed Continental wall tiles

Crackle-glazed tiles and relief border and corner tiles are combined with moulded seashell relief tiles in a range of subtle greens. Use them for kitchen splashbacks and countertops, shower enclosures, bathroom panels, etc.

Hand-decorated glazed wall tiles

The seaside motifs are in clear colours on an antique white ground. They have a light, "fresh" appeal.

Hand-painted, embossed glazed tiles

Three tiles build up to form a combination panel which can be used for dados; to drop into a panel of plain field tiles for walls; or as an inset in a traditional fireplace. The teardrop design is reminiscent of Art Nouveau.

Italian hand-decorated glazed clay wall tiles

These tiles have an Art Nouveau pattern and are combined with ridged and patterned border tiles at the base and a patterned border at the top to form a slim decorative panel for bathroom walls.

American hand-crafted terra clay tiles
A rustic Irish thistle border surrounds mottled green field tiles. These are suitable for floors and countertops and are also frostproof so could be used in a patio area.

Natural antiqued stone
These tiles are set in typical tessellated style to form a panel which could be a centrepiece for a floor or wall area, or form a classical repeating pattern.

Hand-crafted mosaic field and border tiles
These tiles can be used for interior walls in conservatories, halls, kitchens, bathrooms, etc., and exterior walls for pools, patios, roof terraces, fountain splashbacks. The ribbons on the border tiles have a silver lustre finish which produces a weathered patina, ideal for outdoor settings.

Natural stone mosaic border and field tiles
Here, a lotus mosaic border is used to outline diamond-set antiqued stone slabs, ideal for countertops, floors, walls, conservatories and around swimming pools.

Hand-crafted mosaics
This jumping fish mosaic, set into a sea-green border panel, can be used on floors, walls, countertops, pools, conservatories or patios.

Mosaics have been appreciated since ancient times and have an undeniable elegance. They look especially good in "watery" settings and raised relief borders frame them perfectly.

American lustre-glazed wall tiles
Combined with a moulded border tile and topped with a narrow nosing, these tiles create a classically simple, elegant treatment for kitchens, bathrooms and utility area – even hall dados.

Rustic terracotta floor tile and embossed border
The embossed vine border and square corners outline the plain terracotta tile to form a distinctive classical look.

Relief-decorated frieze
The bear, fruit and branch motif is offset by plain glazed tiles and would be ideal to create a traditional tiled dado.

Glazed ceramic wall tiles
Mix and match tile shapes to create an endless variety of patterned borders. The relief liners are used individually rather than joined up for a more unusual look.

American handmade glazed terracotta wall tiles
A leafy hand-painted border is added to plain field tiles, showing how interesting effects can be built up using plain, patterned and moulded tiles – all it takes is a little imagination!

Glazed terracotta tiles
The theme here is Celtic. A raised relief lion and stag are surrounded with small square mosaics and edged with Celtic knotwork. Larger panels could be built up and used to create stunning features for a conservatory.

MOODY
BLUES

BLUE IS THE COLOUR OF PEACE AND HARMONY. IT CAN BE
USED TO CREATE A CALM, RESTFUL AMBIENCE AND
TO BALANCE AN OVER-BRIGHT ROOM. BLUE
ALSO HAS A SPACE-MAKING QUALITY
WHICH CAN ENLARGE A SMALL
ROOM VISUALLY, ALTHOUGH
THE DEEPER TONES ARE
MORE ENCLOSING. ITS
COMPLEMENTARY
COLOUR IS
ORANGE.

BLUE
TILE
DIRECTORY

Blue is the colour of peace and harmony. It is also associated with chivalry, romance, devotion and loyalty. In heraldry it symbolizes piety and sincerity; in mythology it is the colour of the sky gods Jupiter, Juno and Mercury. The rich blues seen in paintings and illuminated manuscripts from the Middle Ages were made using a precious natural pigment and reserved for the Virgin Mary's mantle, often enhanced with gold.

Blue can create a calm, restful ambience and is reputed to lower blood pressure, the pulse rate and brain waves; it can be particularly effective when used in the paler values in hospitals or schools. The deeper tones of blue suggest the velvety richness of a night sky or the infinite depth of the ocean, and seem more enclosing. Most blues (especially the blue-greens) can be chilly or even icy unless they are combined with some of the warmer tones in the spectrum — for instance, terracotta, apricot or burnt-orange (the complementary colour of blue).

Blue is a cool, receding colour and has a space-making quality which helps to enlarge small rooms visually. Blue also has a fairly low reflectance value so it will diffuse and soften strong light — for instance, the paler values of blue will calm an over-bright or very sunny room. The bolder shades can be strident, so it may be best to confine them to accents and accessories, or use them to add depth and contrast to a pale scheme. Specific blues can be used to create a particular

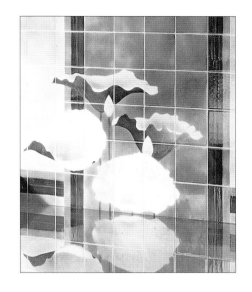

period flavour. Delft and Wedgwood blues, in the seventeenth and eighteenth centuries respectively, were teamed with rich woods, pewter and silver, contrasted with white, and offset with warm-coloured fabrics — a look easy to copy today for a stylish, traditional setting. Blue and white is also associated with the oriental style (the Willow Pattern), which can be replicated by mixing with pale woods, bamboo and lacquer reds. Paler, faded blues used with creamy white, yellow, gold and distressed paintwork and/or furniture suggest a slightly shabby chic Swedish Gustavian theme. A particular shade of grey-blue is synonymous with Shaker style on tiles, floors, woodwork and furniture.

Wall tiles in a strong turquoise, blue-green or sky-blue contrasted with terracotta floor carrés and touches of ochre and sunny yellow suggest the Mediterranean style and add dramatic impact to a hallway or dining room. A kitchen, too, could benefit from this treatment.

Misty and lilac-blues are colours of romance and work well in bedrooms and bathrooms teamed with soft sweet-pea colours. Alternatively, use these blues to decorate a small, sunless room, combined with touches of deep golden yellow, to create a calm, "studious" ambience in a study or home office.

Cleanliness and freshness are synonymous with blue — e.g. the colour of swimming-pool tiles. Blue combined with green creates an even fresher feel — but there must be enough tonal contrasts in the scheme to make it work.

Natural textured quarried slate
The deep blue-grey offsets the complementary burnt orange, set diamond-fashion. Use for floors, inside and out, and seal with special slate sealant.

Hand-painted glazed clay wall tiles
Build up a bold, strong overall design in geometric patterns – use carefully in small spaces or where the tiles need to be cut awkwardly, as this could be visually disturbing.

Italian glazed wall tiles
In plain, richly coloured glazes and coordinating graphic linear pattern, these tiles can be combined to suggest a modern minimalist theme.

Glass mosaics
These mosaic tiles will make a beautiful wall or floor decoration. The various values of blue can be combined to create very different and subtle effects.

Although blue is a cool colour, the range of tones available – from palest blue, through turquoise, to lilac blues, cobalt and dark navy – can produce amazingly different effects.

Hand-crafted moulded tiles
The central poppy tile will produce an original effect on walls, fireplaces, etc. It is set in a simulated mosaic styling of blue-grey field tiles, laid diamond-fashion.

Italian hand-decorated glazed wall tiles
These tiles form a bold geometric pattern. This type of pattern can be grouted in a strong colour to link with one of the colours in the tiles for extra definition.

Italian matt-glazed clay tiles
These tiles can be used to form a distinctive chequerboard pattern with plain coordinating field tiles, or as borders or panels.

Hand-crafted moulded tiles
A mini-geometric design border is combined with round nosing and gloss-glazed field tiles in blue-green. The jewel-bright colours in the border enliven the overall effect.

Moulded glazed border and field tiles
The Georgian moulded liner is set above blue-and-white chequerboard field tiles for dado areas, splashbacks, etc.

Machine-made gloss-glazed wall tiles
The blues in different tones have been arranged to add pattern interest to plain blank walls. Mixed blues create a cool colour scheme for a fresh effect in bathrooms and poolside.

Islamic quarry tiles
Four tiles combine to form a workable module which can be repeated across a surface or used as drop-in panels for floors, walls, fireplaces and countertops. The motifs set a Gothic theme.

Hand-crafted moulded rustic tiles
The scarabs, snails and other animals have a mosaic styling and are used as drop-ins. Use on floors (light use), countertops, fireplaces, hearths, walls, exteriors, etc.

Glazed quarry tiles
The rich orangey-red patterned border enlivens the matt-glazed plain field tiles. The beading has a subtle metallic lustre to give an antiqued effect.

Hand-painted glazed wall tiles
The spiralling Persian border in soft pinks and greens on a strong blue ground is typical of William de Morgan's Arts & Crafts colour combinations.

Glazed ceramic tiles
The bright orange and green patterned tiles are coordinated with a deep blue strip border and make an attractive kitchen panel when set amongst matching solid blue field tiles. The corner tiles from the border are used to form the central motif.

Majolica-glazed European terracotta tiles
These distressed border tiles have a subtle off-white crackle-glaze which, together with the yellow and pink flowers, warm up the cooler blues in the design.

Glazed quarry tiles
Plain tiles are combined with decorative and moulded borders – as these have a distinct Arts & Crafts/Edwardian flavour, they are particularly suitable for hall dados in houses of the period.

Many of the most well-known tile designs – such as Delft – are in blue. Blue tiles on a white background have a clean, classic elegance which is hard to match.

Hand-printed floor and wall tiles

Create a bold border effect with these tiles to enhance a traditional theme. They are strong blue and soft green on pale bone-coloured glaze and can be laid in many combinations.

Spanish glazed clay tiles

These tiles are wood-fired to a traditional European method used for over 2000 years. A blue braided border surrounds crackle-glazed field tiles, set diamond-fashion. They are suitable for walls, countertops and floors.

Stoneware mosaics

These come on an easy-to-handle flexible mesh backing. The soft blue and cream flowing lotus border is used to outline square-set antiqued stone slabs. Use them for countertops, floors, walls, conservatories, pool sides, as panel insets in walls and floors – or use the border mosaics to trim walls and floors.

Majolica-glazed terracotta tiles

These tiles can be used to create panels, frames or to outline features on floors (light use; not outside in cold countries) and walls. The effect of the deep blue leaf border is softened by the juxtaposition of turquoise.

Glazed ceramic wall tiles

An interesting effect is created by combining a marble patterned border with highly glossed nosing on either side.

Portuguese hand-painted wall plaque

Use this classic blue and white border to frame house names and numbers or company names which can either be painted on tiles or some other surface. Try hand-painting or stencilling your own!

Mexican glazed wall tiles

This pretty panel features two bluebirds and a butterfly amongst blue and orange flowers and olive green leaves. The border acts as a picture frame.

American hand-decorated faience-glazed terracotta tiles

In classic blue and white, these wall tiles can be used to create an overall pattern or as a distinctive border.

Spanish glazed clay wall tiles

Combined with a decorative border in blues and greens, incorporating copper glaze for extra shine, these tiles will create a Gothic effect. Use on walls or fireplaces for authentic architectural detail.

Moulded glazed wall tiles

The jewel-bright sapphire blue is stunning. "Ribbon" effect tiles are combined with a moulded rope border and liners, and could be used as a dado trim on a wall of plain or patterned tiles.

Machine-made, screen-printed glazed tiles

Use these tiles as a splashback or feature panel as is, or adjusted to create an attractive border/frieze effect.

Hand-decorated ceramic tiles

Use these tiles as drop-in panels or in a larger grouping to create a bold geometric effect.

A range of floral designs – as borders, central motifs or large patterned panels, they will always look stunning.

Screen-printed glazed tiles
This decorative 12-tile panel of blue posies on a white ground was inspired by a Victorian botanical etching. There are endless design possibilities for kitchens, bathrooms, utility areas, showers, etc.

Portuguese hand-decorated glazed ceramic wall tiles
Four tiles build up to form a decorative panel which can be used as a drop-in or on a wall of plain tiles, or to create an overall effect – this four-tile module could be hung across a wall to form a distinct trellis pattern.

Glazed wall tiles
This relief tile in sapphire blue would look perfect as an occasional drop-in tile on a plain wall or to create a textured border.

Handmade glaze-fired wall tiles
Nine tiles build up into a bouquet of white daisies in a terracotta pot on a deep cobalt blue ground. Match coordinating tiles with a single central motif.

Hand-crafted glazed tiles
Swimming fish, set into a mosaic background, can be combined with blue grout for a realistic sea theme.

Glazed wall tiles
These tiles are designed to be used as a border or frieze and are painted with reproductions of original Arts & Crafts tiles designed by William de Morgan in the 19th century. This colourful fish frieze has fish swimming in a blue river with the swirling leaves forming part of the pattern.

Hand-decorated glazed tiles
Build up an appealing ginger and white cat on a blue and white chequerboard floor, surrounded with 12 plain coordinating glazed tiles to form a frame. Use it as an eye-catching feature on a blank wall.

Spanish glazed clay tiles
Blue fish "swim" across the tiles and are combined with a simple striped border and shell corners. A blue grout would define the pattern more clearly.

American hand-crafted glazed relief tiles
Combine these tiles with flat ones, in stoneware or terracotta for floors and walls, both inside and out (stoneware is frostproof) – for poolside, conservatory or where a shellfish image is appropriate.

Hand-painted wall panel
These are a few of the many nautical-themed tiles available. Patterns can be made up for walls, light flooring, countertops, fireplaces, etc.

These tiles show a wide range of pictorial motifs which are available in blue, from sea-themed designs to country houses.

Hand-decorated, glazed wall tiles

These fruit and vegetable motifs can be used, combined with matching border tiles, to build up a mural; as a random pattern; to create a patchwork effect; or as drop-ins in a wall of plain field tiles.

American faience-glazed terracotta wall tiles

A panel is built up from nine tiles to form mythological sun and moon faces with a decorative circular border. Set it into a wall of blue and white field tiles.

Brazilian handmade, hand-decorated glazed tiles

These Delft-style tiles are made from wet clay using a 17th-century Dutch technique. They have an authentic look and can be used around fireplaces, stoves and in kitchens and even dairies.

Hand-painted border and picture tiles

The whimsical sun and moon design in complementary warm yellow and orange is set against a brilliant blue background. Here, they are set as a panel which could decorate interior walls in household and commercial situations.

Glazed wall tiles

These tiles are combined with moulded border tiles and nosings. The blue and yellow combination sets a sunny scene.

NEUTRALS AND NATURALS

TRUE NEUTRALS ARE PURE WHITE, BLACK AND GREY.
ACCEPTED NEUTRALS ARE COLOURS ASSOCIATED
WITH NATURAL MATERIALS AND FIBRES, AND
"TINTED" WHITES. THESE COLOURS ARE
SOFTER AND EASIER TO USE THAN
BLACK AND WHITE, AND CAN
ENHANCE A SCHEME BY
OFFSETTING RICH, WARM
COLOURS. THEY CAN
ALSO BE USED
ON THEIR
OWN.

NEUTRAL AND NATURAL

TILE DIRECTORY

Neutral and natural colours are, strictly speaking, not colours at all – i.e., they are not made by mixing hues together and do not appear on the colour wheel. In interior design, neutral and natural colours usually provide a link in, or the definition to, a colour scheme, but can also be used on their own. Neutrals often form the background to a patterned fabric, flooring or wallcovering, or are used for a "field" tile.

Neutrals can be divided into two groups: true and accepted neutrals. True neutrals are pure white, black and various values of pure grey, made by mixing black and white together in varying proportions to achieve different tones. Used alone, white and grey

can be cold, stark and uninviting, and black tends to be sombre as it absorbs light, so it needs to be combined with an interesting surface texture. Black, white and grey are discussed in a separate section.

Accepted neutrals are the colours associated with natural materials and fibres – for instance, jute, burlap (hessian), flax, seagrass, sisal, rush matting, natural stone and wood. They include beiges, creams, off-whites, fawns, taupes, mushroom, magnolia and soft browns, and are all easy on the eye and comfortable to live with. However, they can also be bland and safe if they are not enlivened with some bold accents and strong textural contrasts.

"Tinted" whites are also accepted neutrals and are found in most paint ranges, as field tiles and as the background to coloured patterns. All the accepted neutrals relate to the original hues in the spectrum and are very pale values of the pure colour made with the addition of white. For instance, there are peach and pinkish beiges, yellow creams, bluish off-whites, grey-greens and blue-greys. All these neutrals need very careful colour-matching.

The colours of natural materials and fibres are much softer and easier to use than black, white or grey. They can contribute a slightly weathered or aged look to a scheme, or suggest a subtle "shabby

chic" ambience. Select neutrals to enhance the theme – creamy or yellowish neutrals to offset rich, warm colour schemes (chestnut brown, Indian reds, terracotta, gold and ochre) and cooler beiges and "greiges" with the bolder blues and greens.

These colours can also be used on their own to create a relaxing scheme. However, it is important to choose from the same colour palette to avoid a disturbing clash and to vary the tones. It is essential to achieve a really good textural contrast with shiny, rustic, silky, matt, rough, shaggy and sheer light-filtering surfaces.

Italian matt-glazed clay tiles
In a choice of solid colours – black, greys, whites and neutrals – these tiles are cut in a triangular shape and set to form a diamond trellis effect. They can be used for floors, walls and fireplaces.

Unglazed vitrified floor tiles
These 19th-century-style floor tiles are used to recreate an Edwardian style floor, ideal for restoration work or in period buildings for halls, verandahs, porches, etc.

Natural riven slate tiles
Multicoloured slate has a natural veining and can be installed either side up to allow emphasis of the attractive natural shading. They can be used for floors inside and out, as they are slip-resistant in wet areas and thus good for shower rooms and poolside.

Italian quarried limestone flagstones
With natural fossils embedded in the stone, these tiles give a timeless, traditional feel. For residential floors, they must be sealed with a penetrating non-slip sealer.

Unglazed terracotta floor tiles
These tiles can be laid in a variety of ways to create traditional effects and combined with borders to outline features or to define the shape of the room.

Neutrals and naturals work perfectly with every colour in the spectrum. They can be used in simple geometric designs or with detailed patterns – either way, they will never appear overdominating.

Natural floor tiles
The pale cream border tiles are ideal for emphasizing the richly coloured insets. The range of natural materials is enormous and the different types can be laid together, as here, or used to create a tonal colour scheme.

Natural slate floor tiles
Rows of natural-coloured diamonds are coordinated with square orange and red tiles which are simply stronger shades of the diamonds' colour.

Italian mosaics and antiqued stone
Laid in diamond chequerboard fashion, these tiles create a look of timeless elegance for walls, floors, countertops, hearths, etc. This type of treatment will increase the apparent width and size of narrow corridors and small floor areas.

Unglazed vitrified floor tiles
These 19th-century tiles are combined with geometric cut tiles from a range of neutral and deep rich colours. Here, they are used to create the look of an authentic Victorian encaustic floor.

Hand-decorated glazed clay wall tiles
This East wind motif border pattern can be used to trim the top of a plain wall, or individually as drop-ins with a ceramic soap dish decorated to match.

Hand-decorated glazed tiles
A Delft-inspired figurative tile is set into a panel of neutral field tiles which can be used to make a feature of a large, open wall.

Hand-painted glazed tile
A vividly coloured fish painted onto a glazed tile is set into tumbled botticino marble to add colour interest to a natural creamy wall or floor surface.

Hand-crafted glass mosaics
Waterfowl – geese, ducks, drakes and gulls – are depicted on a mosaic wall panel. Mosaics can be used to create a *trompe l'oeil* effect for pools and fountains.

English hand-decorated glazed tiles
Four tiles are used to form a mural depicting a friendly cow in a harvest field. Mural panels can be used to drop into a wall of field tiles, or as an integral part of a splashback or behind a stove or sink.

American hand-decorated glazed porcelain wall tile
This tile depicts an array of seashells. It can be used to form a border, a definite pattern or as random drop-ins.

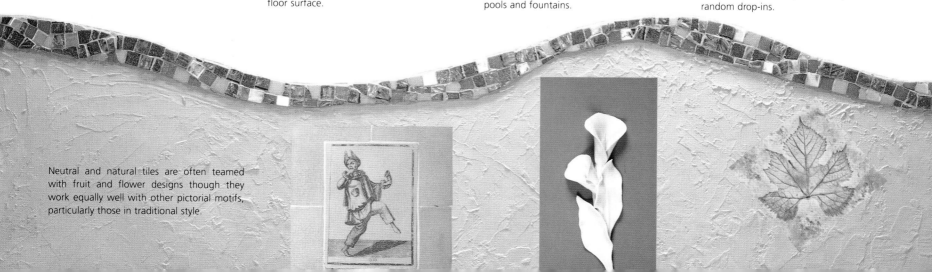

Neutral and natural tiles are often teamed with fruit and flower designs though they work equally well with other pictorial motifs, particularly those in traditional style.

Natural stone tiles
The mood here is ancient Greece and Rome, with figurative scenes drawn to give a *trompe l'oeil* effect, echoing classical sculpture.

Traditional slate tiles
These pewter-grey tiles produce a clean, minimalist look. The ridged nosing and Greek-key border add a touch of decoration to what may otherwise be too cold a look.

Handmade raised-pattern wall tiles
The different fruit patterns stand out in relief against a high-glaze off-white background. Here, the tiles are set into a panel, interspersed with a plain off-white base tile and framed with coordinating border and corner tiles.

Glazed ceramic wall tiles
White tiles are given a touch of warmth and sparkle with a combination of neutral and brightly coloured diamond insets. The fruit border sets a Bacchanalian theme.

Polished marble tiles
Trompe l'oeil pictures of fruit are set into square marble tiles and topped with a fruit border.

Clay wall tiles
This range of plain, textured relief and patterned tiles would look good in any room. The brown and cream tones work very well with ethnic designs and earth colours.

Textured glazed wall tiles
These tiles have a classic, timeless look. It is possible to build up wall features, panels, dados, alcoves, frames and architraves from a range of heavy relief, neutral-coloured tiles.

Hand-cut stone and marble mosaics
These mosaics are set into a classical Greek-key border design to give architectural definition to a grand hall, dining and living room, or conservatory floors.

Natural stone and marble mosaics
Mosaics afford wonderful creative design possibilities. Terracotta, soft pink, white, grey and black mosaics are used to form a classical pattern of rope and Greek-key borders for walls and floors.

Traditional marble mosaics
Natural/neutral colours can be combined to create a typical Romanesque effect for walls and floors in older-style properties or for swimming pools, conservatories and patios.

Antiqued stone with limestone and quarried slate
Random-size small travertine stones are combined with bar liners to create borders, frames and patterns.

"Biblical" stone tiles (over 500 years old from Israel)
Here, Roman stone is set with a Roman border in classical chain-link pattern. Use these tiles for floors and walls, both inside and out, where a characteristic traditional textured look is required and grout in a pale colour for maximum effect.

Antique stone with limestone and quarried slate
Small travertine stones are set brick-pattern and combined with relief and slim rail liners for a subtle yet sophisticated effect.

Antiqued stone with limestone and quarried slate
Creamy travertine stones are combined with limestone and quarried grey slate to suggest a *trompe l'oeil* border for a classical treatment.

Small scale tiles and mosaics in neutral colours are combined with earth tones and jewel-bright splashes for maximum effect. The plain colours and square shapes are contrasted with star bursts, triangles and octagons to play visual geometric "tricks."

Antiqued stone with limestone and quarried slate

The natural colours of limestone contain warm pinkish tones, which is offset with a slate-grey triangular geometric border, topped with a bullnose bar liner.

Natural marble and limestone tiles

Square creamy white tiles have small greige diamond insets to provide pattern interest and are bordered with random-cut limestone to create a softly flowing geometric design.

Hand-crafted moulded glazed tiles

Set in a diamond fashion, these tiles provide a unifying design concept for internal walls, countertops, splashbacks, showers, fireplaces, etc. Some of the tiles have crackle glazes, which are not suitable for very wet situations or countertops.

Natural stone tiles

In natural/neutral colours, these tiles form a random geometric pattern which is ideal for floors, walls and countertops. They can be sealed with beeswax for a rich patina.

Aegean mosaics

This classical circular motif with a cream-coloured leafy image makes maximum use of the natural beige and greenish tones of Aegean mosaics.

Glazed ceramic wall tiles
Cool grey and white glazed tiles are cut to form triangles and narrow borders, offset by basic square tiles outlined with white grout. They are ideal for hot bathrooms and kitchens.

Italian marble floor tiles
Textured tiles are set as a squared panel for use in conservatories or around swimming pools – anywhere that a traditional rustic look will be in keeping with the decorating and architectural style.

Natural quarried slate
Riven slate does not have to be laid in traditional brick or edge-to-edge fashion. Here, green and olive slates are cut to create texture and pattern interest without being too bold in design terms.

Antiqued stone and travertine
Warm beige stone tiles are laid brick pattern and defined by a braided mosaic liner in blue and terracotta at the top and a simple geometric strip below.

Italian glazed floor and wall tiles
Creamy-neutral field tiles are trimmed with a hand-decorated border and corner tiles in crisp clear colours. Use them to create panels, or to outline features on floors and walls.

Natural quarried slate
Slate floor tiles in creamy gold and grey tones are unique as they are a natural quarried material. Triangles are framed with slim rail liners to create a formal pattern.

Natural quarried slate
Calibrated natural slate has a slightly rough textured surface for safety (non-slip). Here, grey-green slate looks lighter when teamed with a pale grey grout.

Borders, frames and chequerboard effects can be created using natural materials and neutral colours with tonal contrast. The effect will be more subtle and softer on the eye than similar patterns made with dark, bold or bright, contrasting colours.

Antiqued stone
Mini-random pattern in light travertine looks like a mature sunwarmed stone wall, trimmed with a starburst border outlined in darker toffee-coloured slabs.

Antique terracotta blonde slabs
This reclaimed material is usually over 150 years old and will have wear layers on some slabs. Use them for floors and walls to achieve a Provencal style, and on patios and verandahs in warm climates.

Aegean mosaics and acid stone slabs
The stylized fish border swims around the central panel, but there are endless permutations combining these mosaic borders with slate, travertine and other stone slabs for individual decorative effect Use them for walls, countertops, pools, etc. They are frostproof and skid resistant so they can be used outside and in commercial situations.

Antiqued stone travertine slabs
These tiles create a classic, aged architectural effect and are trimmed with mosaic borders for extra colour. Use for walls, floors, countertops, pools, showers, etc. They are ideal for outside use as they are frostproof.

Antiqued stone
Set on the slant, the intricate pattern of these tiles creates a feeling of depth. They are ideal where a monochromatic effect will offset a scheme in neutral colours.

BLACK
AND
WHITE

BLACK ABSORBS LIGHT; WHITE GIVES MAXIMUM REFLECTION.
A MIDDLE-TONE GREY WILL TAKE ON A LITTLE OF THE
COLOUR IT LIES NEXT TO. BLACK AND WHITE CAN
BE DIFFICULT TO USE, BECOMING TOO OVER-
POWERING OR TOO GLARING, BUT WHEN
USED CAREFULLY, PARTICULARLY
WITH SHADES OF GREY, THEY
CAN CREATE AN
UNSURPASSED
CLASSICAL
ELEGANCE.

BLACK AND WHITE

TILE DIRECTORY

Black, white and grey are true neutrals (see NEUTRALS AND NATURALS). They do not appear on the colour wheel. Grey is made by mixing black and white together in varying proportions to achieve different tones. Used alone, white and grey can be cold, stark and uninviting, and black tends to be sombre as it absorbs light, so it needs to be combined with an interesting surface texture.

Black symbolizes darkness and death, and is the colour of penitence, grief, mourning and sadness. It also has negative associations, such as Satan, witchcraft and black magic, and anarchy. However, black cats signify good luck in some cultures, and black clothes are seen as the epitome of glamour, sophistication and elegance.

White is the natural complement to black, symbolizing as it does cleanliness, virginity, innocence and chastity. In heraldry the colour white suggests faith and purity. To the Greeks and Hindus it was the colour of pure water

and in ancient mythology it was associated with the moon goddess. However, a white elephant is a burdensome possession, and the white flag of truce is associated with surrender and disgrace. White is reputed to be the strongest light-reflecting surface there is, although in reality it can be clinical, harsh and stark — even greyish.

Grey is the colour of wisdom and intelligence (e.g. grey matter, éminence grise) and bureaucracy.

It is also the colour of insubstantial gossamer, cobwebs and shadows – and is therefore often associated with uniformity and self-effacing people who fade into the background. It is the colour of drabness, urban landscape and city "concrete jungles." Pure, pale and middle-tone greys have a chameleon-like quality, taking on a little of the colour with which they are used.

Used sparingly, black will sharpen up any colour scheme, but when used excessively it can be overpowering. Black can dazzle or "strobe" – this usually happens with striped or check patterns when white or a strong colour is used with black. White has maximum lightness and a shiny finish gives maximum reflection. White will often cool down a "hot" colour scheme of reds, yellows or oranges, or add a special sparkle to dark, rich colours. Used with blue and a touch of sunny yellow, it creates a traditionally fresh kitchen or bathroom theme; combine it with black for timeless classical elegance. Use white on its own to create a sense of space.

Grey is much more user-friendly and versatile than black as it is less heavy and light-absorbing. Pale and middle-tone greys can be used to accent a dark or rich, warm scheme where white could be too glaring. Mix grey with soft pinks, lavenders, mauves and purples for a sophisticated, elegant scheme; or combine it with fondant pinks, aquamarine, lilac, lemon, coral, sky blue, peach and minty-greens for a more gentle effect. A scheme based on grey with black and white can be very flexible, appearing warm in winter and cool in summer if the right accents and accessories are used with them.

Moulded glazed wall tiles

These tiles are frostproof and suitable for use on inside and outside walls. The patterns are varied, and many different effects can be created, all forming a classical and traditional European look.

Matt-glazed wall tiles

This panel of Spanish-inspired tiles shows how an interesting dado and textured effect can be created with what is virtually a plain self-coloured tile. Not all tiles have a shiny unwelcoming feel.

Textured glazed wall tiles

Shiny glazed or matt white wall tiles have a timeless elegance. The geometric effect is reminiscent of Victorian and Edwardian hall dado design.

American moulded glazed liners

Depicting various neoclassical and traditional architectural themes – from rope, rose, shell, leaf and tassel to Greek key – these tiles can be combined with plain glazed tiles and corners to create panels, dados, etc.

Plain and crackle-glazed wall tiles

Here, a warm white crackle-glazed plain-tile central panel is hung diamond-trellis fashion, and surrounded by a raised leaf border and small beaded border tiles as a concept design.

Hand-crafted moulded tiles

These simple raised border tiles have a stylized star and scroll design and have been moulded to look like old plasterwork.

American moulded relief and smooth-glazed wall tiles

The use of a field tile, rose motif and antique white border featuring a moulded branch can make a subtle wall decoration or splashback.

This range of off-white tiles all have raised designs either on a single tile or as a border. The result is simple and subtle, yet extremely effective.

American moulded and shaped glazed tiles
The sea theme motifs form a dado rail and are combined with classical moulded liners in various depths to build up a highly original dado or panel.

Screen-printed glazed wall tiles
This geometric, linear pattern is achieved by screen-printing and is ideal for a streamlined minimalist or hi-tech look in kitchens, bathrooms, etc.

American moulded glazed clay wall tiles
These tiles are in traditional "celestial" designs of moon, stars, sun and wind in soft antique white. Use them to create a border effect or to drop into a wall of plain glazed field tiles.

Hand-crafted crackle-glazed wall tiles
These tiles are hung in a diamond pattern and interspersed with natural terracotta clay moulded borders, with entwined acanthus and vine leaf or curling ribbon swags reminiscent of the 19th-century Arts & Crafts look. This combination can be used for indoor and exterior walls (a mild climate for the terracotta); the white tile is also suitable for some countertops.

Quarried slate

These tiles are combined with a decorative diamond design border and' white insets to create an eye-catching geometric effect. Such combinations allow many design possibilities.

Hand-painted ceramic wall tiles

These plain black tiles have a range of abstract designs hand-painted in white. Use them as drop-ins in a bathroom to create a bold, modern Metropolitan look.

Lustre-glazed clay tiles

This distinctive diamond design gives the effect of an optical illusion. Use such tiles carefully, particularly in a small room.

Ceramic wall tiles

The white tile has an intricately painted black motif whilst the black tile has the same design as a raised relief which has been glazed to draw it forwards from its surround.

Black tiles are particularly suitable for modern, minimalist interior decors; white tiles provide a superb setting for brightly coloured motifs.

Glazed ceramic wall tiles
Black and white chequerboard tiles are interspersed with a bright array of "appliquéed" farm animals and topped with a raised "cloud" border.

Hand-decorated onglaze tiles
The onglaze technique combined with hand-painting creates an individual look. Here, the "rope" border stencilled design in soft colours on a white ground is combined with white field tiles to form a 15-tile panel, but other colour combinations are possible.

Italian glazed wall tiles
Oblong white tiles are laid trellis-fashion with decorated black and grey insets to produce a lively scatter pattern which would be ideal for a plain or dark area.

Glazed ceramic wall tiles
This panel suggesting stained glass would bring a cheerful ambience into a dark room. Use a coloured grout to emphasize the design created by the various tile shapes.

Hand-painted glazed wall tiles
These tiles are decorated with motifs in clear colours on a white ground. Other designs such as fruits, leaves and flowers can be mixed and matched with these culinary designs.

Mexican hand-cut glazed wall tiles
Suitable for bathrooms, showers and kitchens, these tiles are combined with fruit designs. Here, variation is created by inserting some of the tiles diagonally.

Handmade unglazed encaustic tiles
These stylized animal motif tiles create an attractive panel or border effect – they would be great fun on the floor, or as a changing-table top in a child's room.

American hand-moulded glazed wall tiles
These tiles are used to create a concept panel with chequerboard border tiles, combined with plain field tiles, for walls and splashbacks.

Clay wall and floor tiles
Black, blue-grey and off-white tiles are joined with lighter grey grout. The geometric star design would look good in a conservatory or large hall.

Handmade unglazed encaustic tiles
Simple geometric patterns can be formed with combinations of these triangular tiles. They can be used on floors, walls, countertops (if sealed), fireplaces, splashbacks, etc.

Stone and glazed ceramic tiles
The matt stone provides a good visual foil to the rich green tiles. Combining different materials can produce interesting, attractive and often unusual results.

Tumbled marble tiles
These tiles can be used to build up interesting geometric effects on both walls and floors. Use them to add cool Mediterranean character and style.

Italian hand-painted wall tiles
Create a classical octagonal/inset look using a square module, topped with a slim diamond-patterned border for dados and splashbacks.

"Be bold" is the order of the day here. 1920s motifs, geometric designs, dalmatian spots – all of these black-and-white designs could be a stand-out feature in any room.

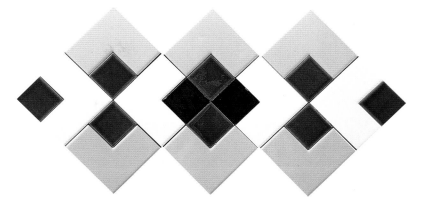

Ceramic wall tiles
Black and prussian blue tiles are combined here with a white and grey background. The light-reflecting surface of the tiles would look good in a small bathroom.

Spanish copper-glazed clay wall tiles
These tiles are laid in chequerboard pattern and topped with an egg-and-dart moulded border in solid colours, and a chain-link decorated lower border.

Matt-glazed clay wall tiles
Solid white and stone grey field tiles are laid diamond-fashion with a raised relief white border which has the effect of a picture frame. The central tile panel could be used on a wall or work surface.

Glazed ceramic wall tiles
Stars and diamonds are given a sumptuous treatment by the addition of a thin gold inlay. The use of star insets rather than square ones gives an Islamic feel to the trellis design.

SHIMMERING
METALLICS

METALLICS USUALLY HAVE AN ATTRACTIVE GLEAM AND
A RICH SURFACE. GOLD, BRASS AND COPPER ARE
WARM; SILVER, PLATINUM AND PEWTER HAVE A
COOL QUALITY. A METALLIC SURFACE
INCREASES THE STRENGTH AND
EFFECT OF A COLOURED TILE
AND CAN IMPROVE A
ROOM WITH RICH
OPULENCE OR COOL
SOPHISTICATION.

METALLIC

TILE DIRECTORY

A "metallic" is, strictly speaking, not a colour but a specific type of shiny texture which can be applied to almost any colour. It is usually created by using metal oxides with pigment to make glazes, inks and dyes for use on wall tiles and painted surfaces and for printing on wallcoverings and fabrics.

This type of texture is usually light-reflecting, with an attractive glint or gleam which makes the surface look brighter, richer, stronger and more "important," and it makes any pattern stand out. As with bold colours, shiny metallic effects can be disturbing and distracting, and should be used with care.

Gold, brass and copper can be classed as warm, and they work in a similar way to the advancing colours of the spectrum. Real gold and gold leaf are, of course, costly and precious; however, gold can now be simulated in paints and glazes. Brass and copper are far less costly than gold and can also be recreated using pigments and glazes.

In contrast, silver, platinum, steel, pewter and chrome have a coolness — in some cases, an almost icy effect — which relates to, and works in a colour scheme in a similar way to pale grey. They tend to recede, and their shiny surface reflects light, visually increasing the apparent size of a space.

Gloss-glazed wall tiles
These can be combined with coordinating plain, similarly glazed field tiles to form a pattern, border or as drop-ins.

American glazed tiles
The metallic "oilslick" look produces sophisticated wall treatments. The snail and shell raised motif is astonishingly realistic – will they leave a shiny trail?

Handmade glazed wall tiles
Bronze autumnal colours are inset with relief-decorated tiles depicting frogs, toads, turtles, lizards, chameleons and fish, with a delicate tracery of leaves on other tiles to create an almost fossilized look. Use as drop-ins or to form a regular pattern; the frog-and-vine makes an effective border design.

Moulded glazed motif tiles
These border tiles are glazed with a rich bronze and golden metallic finish. They can be used to create decorative edging or framing, or combined with other tiles to form panels, dados, etc.

Whether combined with modern abstract patterns, used to create a *trompe l'oeil* effect or treated to give a fluid oilslick look, metallic tiles are an eye-catching feature.

Glazed ceramic tiles
The pattern forms a textured medallion design associated with classical European architecture. They can be used on interior or exterior walls (though not in a cold climate), fireplaces, etc., for dramatic light-reflecting effect.

Italian glazed wall tiles
These tiles create a mosaic effect in "designer" colours. Here, they are set diamond-fashion for dramatic impact.

American glazed wall tiles
Field tiles in jewel-rich colours combined with shell-shaped relief moulding can be hung to form a bold horizontal effect or used as a border/liner or frame.

Glazed wall tiles
The bronze-bright and jewel-rich colours are combined with square mosaics used as drop-ins to create an exotic effect in bathrooms, bedrooms or commercial situations.

PRACTICAL
POINTERS

SURFACE SELECTION

For a really hardwearing and easy-to-clean surface, tiles are often the sensible option. But tiles can come in several different guises – from carpet and vinyl tiles, to rustic quarries and paving slabs. This book is concerned with "hard" flooring and walling which is usually seen as a permanent or at least long-lasting feature. Bear this in mind when making design and colour choices.

Always make sure the tile you choose is suitable for the job. Floor tiles are stronger, thicker and usually larger than wall tiles. They may have substances added to the clay (limestone or flint chippings, silica, etc.) to make them tougher, and this may add a slight glitter to the texture when the tile has been fired. They are also heavier than many other floorings, or wall tiles, and consequently can create problems if used upstairs in an old property or in a conversion. First make sure the joists are strong enough (and have them strengthened if necessary) to take extra weight. Floor tiles for use in conservatories, porches, verandahs, front paths and patios may need to have a visual link with the main house. They must be frostproof, i.e. fired to a sufficiently high temperature to withstand cold and frost and remove the possibility of cracking or breaking up.

Wall tiles are different from floor tiles. They are generally made of earthenware or white "china" clays and have a decorative (hand-decorated, printed, moulded, etc.) or plain glazed surface. Although there are certain "standard" sizes, they come in a variety of different sizes, and some come in original shapes.

▲ This traditional treatment for a front pathway makes full use of frostproof quarry tiles, laid in a bold geometric pattern. The design could be echoed on the hall floor in this Victorian house.

◀ Venetian marble slabs are laid diamond-fashion to "frame" a curvaceously shaped indoor pool. Floors in such areas must be impervious to water and non-slip.

There are also small "insets" or "drop-ins" which are used as an integral part of designs.

Wall tiles should never be used as flooring because they are not strong enough. In some cases, perhaps where continuity is required, floor tiles can be used on the wall. However, they are heavier, thicker – and so reduce the space – and are often more clumsy. Many manufacturers produce a wide choice of coordinating floor and wall tiles, which could be a better option for a seamless look.

There are also tiles produced specifically to be used as countertops, which are heavier than a simple laminate top. Kitchen, bathroom and bedroom furniture carcasses may therefore need to be strengthened at the joints to take the extra weight. Tiles for countertops must be impervious to oils, acids and other cooking liquids to be hygienic, so do not choose tiles with any porosity or with a "crackle" glaze. In some instances, unglazed floor tiles may be suitable for work surfaces if a special epoxy grout is used and they are properly sealed and maintained – ask the supplier for advice.

Finishes

Highly glazed and glossy tiles, and those with a lustre (shiny) finish, are only suitable for use on walls and some work surfaces, as they would be highly dangerous on floors; the majority of floor tiles are matt or semi-matt for obvious reasons.

Tiles can also be textured for extra visual and tactile interest, and also as an extra safety factor for floors. However, dirt can become trapped in deep indentations and cleaning may be difficult. Floor tiles with a rustic texture are suitable for a country or Mediterranean-style room. Tiles of stone, slate, etc., can have a special riven surface – a slight texturing which makes them non-slip – but again, cleaning may be harder.

DESIGN OPTIONS

As most tiles are a regular shape (usually rectangular or square), there are endless design possibilities with plain colours, before patterned tiles are even contemplated. For example, light and dark coloured floor tiles laid in a chessboard design will always look elegant and will help to make a small floor look larger, and increase the apparent size of the whole room.

Tiles can also be laid to form specific geometric patterns. This may be done by clever placing of plain tiles, or setting them diamond-fashion, or using different sizes to form a border effect to outline a room or salient feature. Tiles can be installed to create striped effects, either horizontally, vertically or diagonally. Tiles can also be cut diagonally to produce triangles, to extend geometric possibilities.

Alternatively, tiles can be set to graduate softly down the wall or across the floor in a monochromatic effect; starting with rows of pale tiles at the top of a wall, and working down to darker tones of the same colour, can be a very stylish treatment. A patchwork effect using single, or even old tiles, can create an

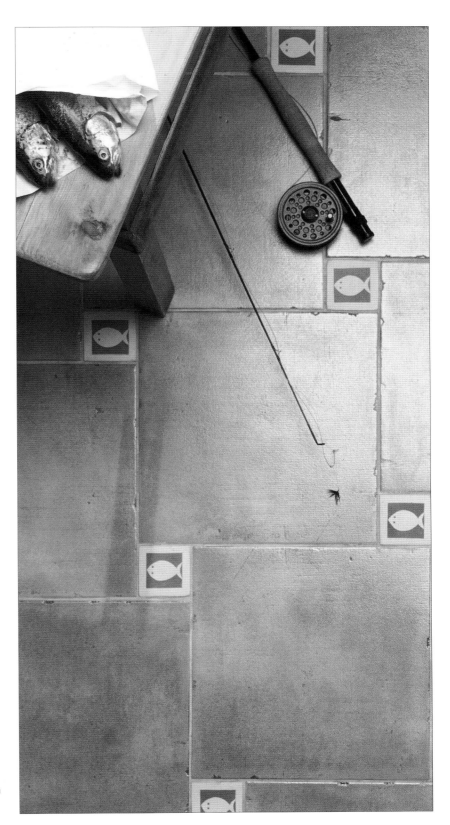

▷ Small encaustic insets add interest to plain glazed floor tiles in a farmhouse kitchen.

◁ Plain tiles can be used to create amazing geometric patterns. Such designs work best on a large, unbroken area of wall or floor.

unusual feature. Always try to combine tiles from the same range, or at least from the same manufacturer. If this is impossible, make sure the thickness and weight is uniform.

Tiles are individually produced. Many handmade and hand-decorated tiles, or those with a dense colour, can have slight variation in tone and/or colour from different firings. It is therefore essential to get the tiler or flooring contractor (or you if you are doing it yourself) to "shuffle the pack." Open all the boxes or pallets and use the tiles at random, so any inconsistencies are lost when spread across a large area.

Pattern – and Plain

Tiles come in a baffling selection of designs and colours. Border and motif tiles can be set at the top, or across an area of plain tiles, or used to outline a salient feature. Motif tiles can be placed randomly throughout a run of plain or textured tiles for extra visual interest (although this often does not look as exciting as hoped!).

Tiles can also be produced to build up a pattern to cover an entire area, and can be floral, geometric, narrative, etc., or have a particular "period" flavour. Choose these to suit the architectural and decorative style of the room (some ranges are produced to coordinate specifically with wallcoverings and fabrics). There are also sets of tiles which form a complete picture, known as "panels." They may be sold already boxed, or made to order. Panels can make an interesting feature on a blank wall, and work particularly well in a windowless bathroom. Mural patterns can also be designed to order and look very effective around a swimming pool, in a dreary hall or in a commercial situation.

Most plain tiles have a solid-colour effect created by the glaze, or are composed of a natural material which gives its own colour to the tile. There are a wide variety available

Be Bold with Borders

Some tiles are specifically designed to be used as borders to "neaten" or create a "frame" on a plain wall, or to outline and define a feature. They can be strongly geometric [A, B, E] or flowingly floral [C, D]. Choose the pattern to suit the style of the room and the rest of the decorations.

Design a Border using Plain Tiles

Plain tiles can also be cut in a variety of shapes and hung in different ways to add impact and form borders, frames or panels [F, G, H].

A

B

C

D

E

F

G

H

Stylish Shapes for Flooring

The regular module of tiles makes designing a fabulous floor much easier. Shown here are a few possibilities from herringbone and brick effect [C, G, J] to the classic way of combining a square or octagonal tile with a key square as an inset [B, E, F, K]. The tiles can be combined with a border [A] for extra definition, and can be laid in a diamond-trellis fashion [F, I, K]. Lozenge-shaped tiles [D, H] look dramatic even if they are laid in a conventional way.

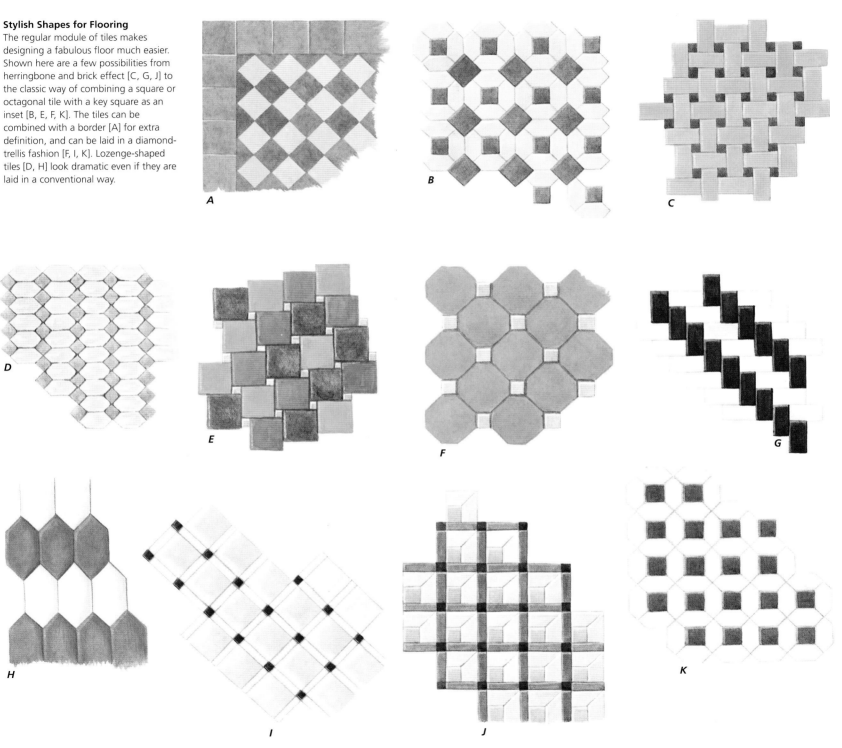

which allows many design possibilities. Many stippled, marbled, dragged, water-splashed and shadow-stripe effects are produced as an alternative to solid colour to create a slightly larger effect – they are good for walls in a small bathroom.

Look before you Leap

Remember that bold designs and strong colours seem more intrusive when used over a large wall or floor area. (They can have the visual effect of "falling in" on you or coming up towards you.) The paler colours and softer patterns tend to fade into insignificance and are unobtrusive when used in bulk. Try to follow the colour rule of relating the scale of pattern or strength of colour to the size of the surface on which it is to be used. Showrooms have tile displays, which help you to judge the finished effect, such as pull-out display boards for walls and trays for floors. Special mirrored boxes or mirrored panels help to magnify the effect of several tiles used together, so a whole wall or floor can be assessed.

When selecting tiles, take samples of existing items in the room (bathroom equipment, kitchen cabinets, fabrics, etc.) with you. If this is not possible or practical, ask to take a tile or two home with you to check *in situ*. Look at them on the correct plane – wall tiles against the wall and floor tiles down on the floor – and under exact lighting conditions, both day and night.

◀ A cool blue hand-painted traditional *trompe l'oeil* tile panel would look fresh and elegant in a kitchen, bathroom, hall, dining room or conservatory, adding visual interest without being too overpowering.

◀ Different tones of natural terracotta floor tiles are laid in a diamond design to increase the width of the space visually, and bordered to suggest a rug – a good treatment to break up a long narrow floor area.

PREPARATION – THE UNDERPINNINGS

As with all interior decoration, the finished job will only be as good as the initial preparation. This applies not only to the surface on which you will lay floor tiles, or hang wall tiles, but more essentially to structural problems – damp or dry rot must be dealt with first, for instance. If an area is damp, a permanent floor treatment could form an impervious barrier and cause condensation (rising damp) to creep up the walls, or damp walls may crumble and the tiles fall off!

Hard (permanent) flooring – such as tiles, stone, marble, slate, earthenware *carrés*, etc. – is very heavy. When combined with a large cast-iron bath filled with water, or used in a kitchen with massive units and hefty kitchen appliances, their weight becomes an even more important factor. If this type of floor is contemplated in a conversion, or for an upstairs room in an older property, the floor joists should always be checked first to make sure they can bear the extra weight and, if necessary, be strengthened. In many older properties, floorboards and joists are narrower the higher they are positioned in the house – the servants living in the uppermost rooms were provided with only essential furniture!

When you contemplate tiling a wall or floor area, think carefully about any other work which might be carried out. Installing new lighting may involve embedding cable in the wall, or replumbing can lead to new pipe runs. If possible, do not embed cables or pipes under permanent flooring because if something goes wrong, the whole floor may have to be excavated to find the fault. (There are electronic devices which detect faults, but they are not always accurate.) It is wiser to run cables or pipes around the edge of the floor and conceal them behind panels, or cover with some boxing-in.

When tiling walls, avoid hiding electric cables behind, or having switches and controls combined with, the tiled wall area. To overcome this problem, a panelled "inspection hatch" could be made and tiled to match the rest of the wall. It is also worth adding a panel around the bath or basin, and then tiling it to match the wall area. This creates a neat, seamless look and visually increases the size of the room. These panels need to be constructed so they can be removed easily if you are faced with plumbing problems.

What Goes on Top of What – Walls

Before hanging tiles, the surface must be level, smooth and free from grease and dust. You may be presented with a variety of wall surfaces to prepare:

Plastered walls can usually be tiled. Leave new plaster to dry for at least one month before tiling, and then seal with tile adhesive primer. Old plaster can be sanded and any cracks filled. Allow the putty (filler) to dry before tiling, and if it covers a large area, prime with tile adhesive primer.

Wallboard (plasterboard) can be tiled if it is firm and on a solid framework, but do not use very heavy tiles. Treat as for a plastered or painted wall.

Painted walls can usually be tiled, but may need to be "keyed" first. Make sure the paint is firmly stuck to the wall. Remove any hooks, nails, etc., and pull out any old anchors (wallplugs), fill any holes, and sand any bumps. Any "suspect" area of painted surface (which has been subject to damp, efflorescence, etc., or is flaky or powdery) should be sealed with tile adhesive primer. Use sandpaper to reduce gloss paint to a matte surface, and then wash with sugar soap. Treat latex emulsion paint or distemper similarly, and then, using the corner of a paint scraper, score the entire surface in a 4in (10cm) wide criss-cross pattern. This keyed surface ensures that the adhesive bonds with the wall. Seal with tile adhesive primer if necessary.

Wallpapered walls are unsuitable for tiling (including heavier, embossed papers and painted woodchip paper). All wallpaper must be completely stripped and any cracks filled. Sand the surface and wash with sugar soap and, if necessary, coat with tile adhesive primer. Lining or cross-lining walls is not recommended before tiling.

Panelled walls are usually not suitable for tiling. However, special blockboard or water-and-boil-proof (WBP) plywood panels can be made, for where you want to have access to the wall behind. These need not be beautifully finished but must be stable; any bare wood frame should be primed with oil-based primer.

Wood panelling that has been tiled may not remain stable, so it is best to remove it. Hardboard is too flimsy to tile, and chipboard and insulation board swell when wet. Prepare the area behind the panelling according to its surface (wood cladding is sometimes used to cover old tiles!).

Existing tiles – it is possible to tile on top of existing tiles as long as they are firmly adhered. The wall should be thoroughly checked first – if the new tiles are very heavy, they could pull the old tiles off the wall! If the wall is solid, remove any cracked or loose tiles and level the cavity with putty (filler). "Key" (rub firmly) the surface with a coarse silicon carbide paper and then wash with sugar soap. Tile adhesive used on a previously tiled surface takes longer to dry than on a plastered or painted wall, so leave the tiles for a longer period before grouting (about 3–4 days). In this situation, self-spacing "Universal" tiles with several bevelled glazed edges are practical and easier to hang.

What Goes on Top of What – Floors

In the main, floors should be professionally laid, which means calling in a flooring contractor to advise, estimate and then possibly carry out the work. Many suppliers, importers and manufacturers can recommend suitable contractors, and some will actually do the work. As with all decorating jobs, it is wise to obtain at least two or three estimates. Before booking the work force, ask how long the work will take to carry out, as well as cost; also ask for

◄ Exotic classical patterns on glazed wall and floor tiles create a raised Turkish-style bathing area, reminiscent of the Islamic tiled walls seen in harems and palaces in the Middle East in the 17th and 18th centuries. Young men "doing the grand tour" were inspired by such treatments and copied them when they returned home and refurbished their historic houses and mansions.

recommendations from a few satisfied customers, unless the supplier has suggested the contractor.

Concrete or cement floors can usually be laid directly onto the surface if it is smooth, level and clean. In some cases, for instance if the floor is uneven, floor-leveling compound may need to be applied first.

Direct-to-earth Some older properties do not have suspended floors, and flagstones were usually laid directly on the earth. This can still be done if the area is level and free from damp, although screeding may be more satisfactory. Quarry tiles are usually laid in a mortar bed, so are particularly suitable in this situation.

Wooden suspended floorboards cannot have tiles laid directly on top. Wood can warp, and the tiles could crack with the movement. Wooden floors need to be covered with a ⅝in (15mm) of exterior grade plywood, which will stand up to the moisture in the adhesive. This should be "staggered" so it does not line up with the boards, and if necessary "inspection hatches" should be provided. Some wooden floorings, such as parquet tiles, may already be laid on top of a concrete or cement base; floorboards are usually fixed to wooden joists. It is better to take these up and start from scratch.

Vinyl and linoleum can have tiles laid on top if the original subfloor is in good condition, and the main floor is properly stuck down, and is clean and level. Vinyl and lino must be treated first with a special primer.

Old tiles and flagstones, etc. It may be possible to restore a floor which is already tiled by replacing broken, cracked or worn tiles or stones. If this is not feasible, and you are proposing to completely renew the hard flooring, do not pour floor-leveling compound or a new hard base on top — it is far better to have it taken up professionally for salvage. The reclaimed floor may be exactly what somebody else is looking for, and you will have more in your budget from the sale of the old floor to put towards your new one.

WHEN TO DO IT YOURSELF

When it comes to the actual physical work, it is always best to be realistic and admit your limitations! Tiling a floor is heavy work, but tiling walls and work surfaces are both well within the capability of the average handy person and can be very satisfying to do.

Walls are not particularly difficult to tile and tiling a work surface should be even easier. Your experience, together with the information in this book, will tell you which surfaces you can and cannot tile. So both jobs can be tackled yourself, as long as you remember the following golden rules. Start with a suitable surface – clean, smooth and dry; purchase the right sort and correct number of tiles; use the right tools for the job. Make sure you have the correct quantities of tiles as well as suitable adhesive and grout to finish the job.

Laying Floorings

Tiling floors is heavy work. Bearing in mind this type of hard flooring usually becomes a permanent and integral part of the building, you do not want to make a mistake, and may decide to call in the professionals. A specialist flooring contractor is probably the preferred option, although many builders are qualified to lay most types of hard flooring. Some suppliers of tile, slate, stone, etc., have a supply-design-and-lay service; others can often recommend suitable contractors in your area.

Many of the conservatory, kitchen and bathroom specialists who offer a "package" of design-build-and-install also offer to lay floor tiles and hang wall tiles. Others consider this to be part of the decoration or finishing of the room, and do not include it in their service. Always check to see exactly what is on offer – a quote may be cheaper from one source than another because they do not decorate, hang tiles or lay flooring.

Quarries and some ceramic tiles could be installed yourself, although quarry tiles need to be laid in a mortar bed, which is hard work to prepare. In the main, it is best to leave marble, slate, natural stone, earthenware slabs, flagstones, granite, etc., to be laid by the experts. A professional will also make sure the subfloor is suitable – and if necessary level, re-screed or strengthen it, and should also know the correct adhesives, grout and final dressing to use. If laying a floor yourself, check the right materials to use with the manufacturer or supplier. Do not forget that final dressings should always be non-slip.

When laying a floor yourself, consider your method of working so you do not "box yourself" into the room! You will need to leave the room and shut the door while the tiles "settle," and the mortar or adhesives and grout dry (sometimes this can take about three days). With the design worked out in advance, lay out the tiles accordingly. Always start at the corner farthest from the door and work backwards towards the exit.

▶ An interesting, almost textured, effect is created by the clever use of stoneware floor tiles in warm natural colours. Such a complex design, using weighty tiles, is a job best left to the experts.

Designing Floors and Walls

If you do not have the confidence to design a floor or wall yourself, there are experts who can do it for you. Many tile suppliers and specialist makers and studios will work out individual designs; they can even create and decorate tiles for a unique look or a *trompe l'oeil* mural effect. Some of the specialist contractors, suppliers and manufacturers provide a design service using CAD (computer-aided design), and produce a printout to scale, together with quantities of the tiles needed.

Alternatively, a professional interior designer can take the burden off your shoulders. They prefer to work from the floor up because the floor is one of the most permanent areas in a room, and all other surfaces are seen in relation to it, as well as the furniture standing on it. They usually ask lots of questions to establish your needs and requirements – including the available budget. They will measure and then produce sample boards and plans, and a rough idea of costs. Once you approve the designs, they obtain firm quotes from the suppliers and work force, and then order the materials. Ask them to obtain quotes for the time the job is likely to take, as well as cost. Most interior designers will supervise every stage of structural and decorating work, so if the job is likely to be messy, this may be a wise opportunity to take a short trip away from home!

For a floor or wall which is to have a special pattern or design set into it, the designer will usually submit detailed plans and/or elevations as well as sketches. If you are undecided about the way a specific design will work, ask them to provide some alternative suggestions. The designer will probably provide them on a separate overlay so you can judge the full effect by placing it over the top of the scale floor plan or wall elevations.

PLANNING THE DESIGN

Plan the effect of a tiled area on paper first. This means you can make alterations without making mistakes, and it also helps to work out the quantities of tiles required. If you are having a professionally designed floor or wall installed, the supplier may use CAD (computer-aided design). You may have the opportunity to see the finished effect on screen, and you will be given a printout, together with a list of the quantities of tiles required. Always order a few spare tiles to allow for accidents or mistakes!

However, in the absence of CAD, experimenting on paper can help if you are undecided on a particular effect or way of grouping tiles. Look at these designs in the room which is to be tiled, and discuss them with other family members (if relevant). It may be useful to draw a scale plan of the wall or floor area to be tiled on squared or graph paper, and to try out different effects on tracing paper overlays.

Start by measuring accurately and preparing the basic plans (do this yourself, even if you have an architect's or builder's plan). Make a floor plan: this is a flat plan which represents a room looking down from above. It needs to contain the exact positions of doors (and door "swings" to show which way they open), windows, alcoves, recesses and projections (such as a chimney breast), radiators, built-in furniture, plumbing positions and electric points, etc.

If the walls are to be tiled, make wall elevations for each wall – these are similar flat plans of walls with any important fixtures such as windows, doors, etc., drawn to scale in the correct position. These plans are invaluable for tiling around windows, doors and other features.

Equipment

In order to measure accurately, you will need a 5- or 7-yard (metre) retractable steel tape (fabric tape measures stretch with use!), a plumb line, a spirit level, a T-square, sketch pad, pencils and pens.

To draw the finished plans, you will need a ruler (preferably a scale rule), a set square (to ensure accurate angles), a pair of compasses (to draw curves/door swings), pencils, a drawing pen or good-quality ballpoint, squared or graph paper, and detail or tracing paper for the finished plan and/or overlays.

Measuring

It helps to have another person to assist – to hold the other end of the tape, and perhaps to cross-check your measurements or call them out for you to write down. First sketch a rough plan of the room and the walls – at this stage it does not need to be accurate. Then measure accurately and write the measurements on the plan. Start at one corner of the room and work outwards from it. When measuring, keep the measure taut, and to make sure you have the true vertical and true horizontal, use the spirit level and plumb line. Ideally, take the horizontal measurements at ground level.

Measure the depth and height of baseboards (skirting), dados and dado rails, window frames, depth and width of sills, height of windows from the floor, doors and door frames, window frames, architraves, etc.; mark exact positions of built-in furniture, electric outlets (points) and pipes. Also take diagonal measurements across both walls and floors, to help check the final plan.

Choose a scale to work in, making one square on the paper equal to one unit of measurement, and transfer the measurements from your rough drawing to squared paper. Use a pencil first, and when you are satisfied the plan is correct, draw it in ink. For the **floor plan**, draw the shape of the room accurately in your chosen scale. When working in metric, a scale of 1:25 or 1:50 is usual, but if you are using standard (imperial) measurements, make one foot of floor space equal to 1in or ½in on the paper (i.e. a scale of 1:12 or 1:24). Indicate any projections, recesses, etc. Use the compasses to draw curves (door swings) and the set square for neat angles.

Using the same scale as for the floor plans, draw the **wall elevations** in a similar way. Include the exact

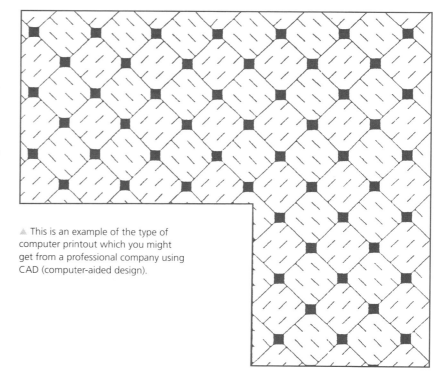

▲ This is an example of the type of computer printout which you might get from a professional company using CAD (computer-aided design).

position of windows, doors, built-in furniture and any items which are seen against the wall, e.g. a sink, kitchen units, bath (allow for any panelling [boxing-in] of such items).

Use this plan to figure out the floor or wall tile pattern. Take several photocopies to use for rough initial planning; you can then trace your design onto plain tracing paper, and use coloured pencils to indicate the finished effect. By using a transparent acetate or tracing paper overlay, you can work out the best way to position the tiles to avoid difficult edges or an awkwardly placed motif. Always centre a pattern or motif on an architectural feature in the same way as you would with wallpaper. When planning a very complicated design, it is worthwhile working to a scale of one square on the paper equal to one tile. With an accurate plan and design completed, you can then figure out the exact quantities of tiles required.

Estimating Quantities

First of all, check the size of tile to be used. There are "standard" square or rectangular tiles, but imported tiles may be of a different shape and size. There are different shapes – octagonal, lozenge, special interlocking shapes and triangular (although it is more usual to cut a square tile across the diagonal if you

▲ Sketch a floor plan and mark on all the relevant measurements. Use a compass to draw the door swings and do not forget to include architectural features.

ESTIMATING QUANTITIES OF TILES REQUIRED

Draw a plan (called an elevation) of each wall. First, multiply the width and height (A) to establish the total area. Do the same to calculate the area taken up by doors (B); windows (C); and other architectural features (D). Subtract these from the total wall area to find the space to be tiled. Divide this by the area of each tile to calculate the number of tiles. Allow for wastage due to awkward areas.

want to use triangles). Border tiles (designed to go at the top of a run of tiles) are usually narrow in depth, but they relate in width to the tiles with which they are used.

Always make sure you buy enough tiles to complete the job, and check that they are from the same "batch" or firing (there is usually a batch number printed on the box); the colour can vary dramatically from one firing to another.

Standard wall tile sizes are 4 x 4in (100 x 100mm); 4¼ x 4¼in (108 x 108mm) – the traditional British bathroom size; 6 x 6in (152 x 152mm); 6 x 8in (152 x 203mm); 8 x 8in (203 x 203mm); 8 x 10in (203 x 250mm); 8 x 12in (203 x 300mm).

There are several *faux* mosaic tile brands available. These are standard-size tiles textured and scored to look like a mosaic and hung as conventional tiles.

Mosaic tiles are much smaller. They can be 1 x 1in (25 x 25mm) or 2 x 2in (50 x 50mm), but they usually come as panels on a fibre-mesh backing. They are installed by embedding the backing into the adhesive or, alternatively, they may have a paper facing which can be removed easily after setting the mosaics in place.

The panels usually measure 10 x 10in (250 x 250mm) or 12 x 12in (300 x 300mm), overall measurements which can be used to calculate quantities.

If the smaller-sized mosaic tiles are not available separately, they can be removed from the backing of a panel and used individually. They can be used as drop-ins to form a "key square" – combined with octagonal-shaped plain tiles, usually in a contrasting colour to add decorative interest – a very traditional way of laying tiles, especially on floors. Always make sure drop-ins and field tiles are designed to be used together – depth, glaze, size, etc., must all be compatible.

Small floor tile sizes are: 6 x 4in (152 x 100mm); 6 x 6in (152 x 152mm) (quarries); 8 x 6in (200 x 152mm); 8 x 8in (200 x 200mm) upwards.

Some stone, slate, etc., tiles can be as large as 10 x 16in (280 x 400mm) or 12 x 12in (300 x 300mm). Older flagstones and reclaimed earthenware tiles can be even larger – up to 18 x 18in (500 x 500mm) and beyond, so always double-check the size of the tiles before you start working out patterns and effects on squared paper, or trying to calculate quantities.

A tiled wall needs neat edges. To half- or part-tile and finish with a border is simple enough. With ordinary square tiles, use fully glazed edges on exposed sides. "Universal" or self-spacing tiles have several bevelled, glazed edges so they can be used for corners and edges.

This problem rarely occurs with floor tiles, as they butt right up to the baseboard (skirting). Where floors join at a doorway, they may need to be combined with a threshold. There are several different types, made from metal or wood. Wooden thresholds can be coloured to coordinate with the flooring, or special slim linking tiles are available.

EXPERIMENTING WITH TILE DESIGNS

Draw a plan of each section of wall to be tiled; ideally, one square will equal one tile.

Draw the design on the plan. Use pencil first so that you can erase mistakes.

CUTTING TILES

Most tiling jobs will involve cutting and possibly drilling the tiles. Wall tiles are fairly easy to cut; floor tiles are harder. Learning to do this takes a little practice, and there may be a few breakages, so make sure you have enough spare tiles to allow for mistakes! Glazed tiles are vitrified, and cut edges can be very sharp, so it is wise to wear gloves when cutting tiles.

Most wall tiles have a glazed surface and are fairly brittle. Once the glazed surface has been scored, the tile should snap easily along the scored line. Mark the glazed side of the tile where it is to be cut using a metal straightedge and then score it with a tile cutter. You should wear protective gloves. Never mark the back of a tile with a felt pen or marker, as the clay can absorb the colour and seep through to the front of the tile. The traditional technique is then to place a matchstick under the back of the tile, level with the scored line, and to press firmly on each side of the tile to achieve a clean cut. Alternatively, a tile-cutting jig has a built-in marking gauge – it should come with full instructions.

To cut a tile to fit around a light switch, window frame or pipe, draw and score the shape in the same way and then "nibble" away the excess with pincers, or use a tile-cutting hacksaw blade. Any rough edges can then be smoothed with a carborundum stone or tile file. To cut a square or oblong shape from the

corner of a tile, first score the outline of the piece to be cut; then score criss-cross lines across the portion of tile which is to be removed – this makes it easier to cut away the excess with pincers or clippers.

Using a tile saw is easier than "nibbling" the tile away with pincers, but it has a very sharp blade. The tile must be supported carefully on a firm surface, with the part to be cut away projecting over the edge. In some cases, it is advisable to use the tile saw in conjunction with a vice or special work bench, in which case the tile should be padded to prevent shattering. Another type of specialist cutter has a cutting wheel to score the glaze, and jaws to hold the tile; when the handles are squeezed, the

jaws close and break the tile. One of the easiest ways to cut a round shape accurately in the centre of a tile is to make a template from brown paper or cardboard first. Trace the outline onto the tile, cut it in half and then "nibble" or cut away the two semicircles to make the hole for a pipe or light switch.

There are specialist profiling tools to help take an impression of difficult shapes; movable plastic or metal "teeth" mould around any shape they are pressed against, to give an accurate guide. This is very useful for awkward moulded architraves, window frames, the sides of a basin, etc. You can use them to draw the shape directly onto the tiles, or to make a template first.

CUTTING OUT SHAPES WITH STRAIGHT EDGES

Score the outer edges of the shape to be cut, then score diagonally across the area.

Use pincers to nibble away the corner. Smooth the cut edges.

CUTTING OUT SHAPES WITH CURVED EDGES

Draw the shape to be cut onto a cardboard template and copy this onto the tile. Score.

Nibble away the curved corner with a pair of pincers and then smooth the cut edges.

CUTTING A TILE INTO TWO PIECES

Use a ruler to score a straight line along the glazed side of the tile with a tile cutter.

Place a matchstick underneath the scored line. Press the edges of the tile to break it.

CUTTING OUT A CIRCLE IN THE CENTRE OF A TILE

Score and break the tile in half. Draw a semicircle onto each half with a template.

Use pincers to nibble away the semicircles. Place the two tiles back together.

DRILLING HOLES IN TILES

Place masking tape over the areas to be drilled to stop the drill from slipping.

If you need to drill a hole in a ceramic tile, do this after the tile is in position. Measure and mark the point to be drilled and stick masking tape over the marks to prevent the bit from slipping. Use a special spade-shaped tile bit on the drill and switch to a low speed; protect your eyes, face and hands from the powdered glaze/glass which flies off.

Floor Tiles

Floor tiles are much harder to cut than wall tiles. An ordinary wall tile cutter cannot be used, although a stout tile saw is adequate for cutting out small pieces (clamp the tile in a vice or special work bench with protective padding). You will need to purchase or rent a special floor tile cutter, or if you are working with thick tiles (quarries, etc.), you will need a professional tile cutter. These can usually be rented from specialist shops, or sometimes from tile suppliers and hardware stores (DIY shops). If renting tools, make sure they come with full operating instructions.

For very heavy tiles and quarries, an angle grinder is the best tool to use and is available to rent. These need careful handling; always wear protective clothing, including boots, and support the tile on a stout surface. Do not put the grinder down until the wheel has stopped.

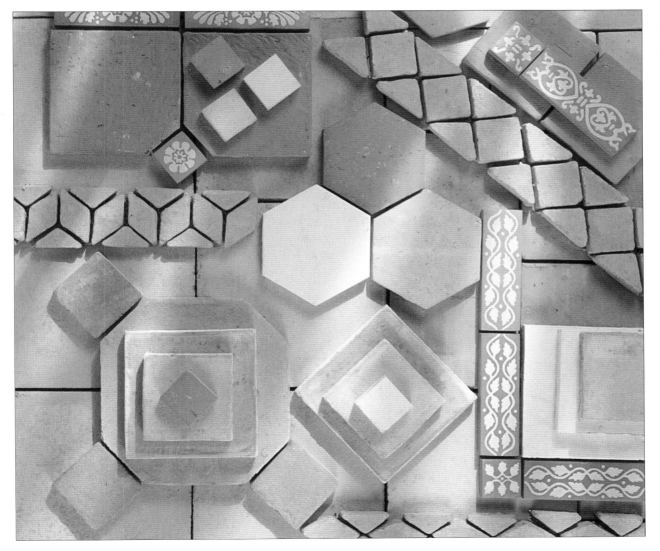

◀ A selection of terracotta tiles in rich earth colours for floors and work surfaces – such tiles are thicker and tougher than wall tiles and are much harder to cut, so this is a job often best left to an expert.

GROUTING TILES

Grout is the essential finishing touch to most tiled surfaces; it prevents water and other liquids and dirt from penetrating the gaps between the tiles. The tiles are grouted after they have been in place for about 12–48 hours (refer to the adhesive package for the recommended time) and the adhesive is set. Grout is usually a neutral colour, but it is possible to purchase coloured grout, or to colour it yourself, if the lines formed by the tiles are intended to be an integral part of the finished design.

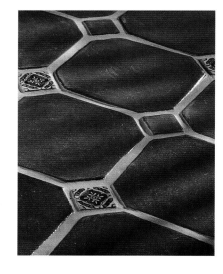

Grout comes either in powder form or ready-mixed in a tub. Powder needs to be mixed in a bucket to a fairly stiff and smooth consistency, according to the manufacturer's instructions. Ready-mixed grout needs to be stirred well, and replace the lid when it is not being used. Make sure you have enough grout, but if you are using powder, do not mix too much if the job is being done in several stages. Work as quickly as possible, as grout hardens rapidly.

There are different types of grout; always make sure you use the right one for the job. For example, a special epoxy grout must be used for countertops because it is impervious to cooking "spills" and acids. This type is also often recommended for floors for hygiene reasons. As grouting can be a messy job, always cover nearby surfaces before starting (bath, sink, kitchen units, etc.). Remove spacers or matchsticks if you have used them. Using a special grout spreader, rubber squeegee blade or damp sponge, spread the grout over the tiled surface. Work quickly, pressing the grout well into the gaps. Do not let the grout harden on the front of the tiles – wipe away any excess with a damp sponge, and wash it out frequently to avoid smears. When using epoxy grout, use a spatular to remove the excess. When the grout has begun to harden, run a rounded stick between the joints to smooth them off and make sure there are no gaps. At the same time, check for any grout left on the tiles and remove it at once. When tiles butt up to an adjoining surface (e.g. a bath, sink, countertop, etc.), do not grout along the joining line; this needs to be sealed with a silicone or acrylic sealant after the grout has dried fully. Scrape out any grout which inadvertently falls into the gap.

The same method is applied when grouting a floor, starting from the corner farthest from the door, backwards towards the exit, and cleaning grout off the top of each tile as you go. As the grout hardens, run a piece of dowel between the joints to firm it in and check there are no air pockets. Leave to harden as recommended by the manufacturer.

When laying quarry tiles, it is best to seal them before grouting. Take advice on which sealant to use (two coats of thinned linseed oil is a popular option); grout and then rub with a coarse cloth. If there are grout stains on the top of the tiles, use sawdust to remove them – strew it over the floor, rub with a damp cloth, and sweep up the residue.

Design Tip

If you are not retiling, you can regrout an existing tiled wall, floor or work surface to give it a new lease of life. A change of colour to define the tiles – to contrast or coordinate with them – can create an important design feature.

STANDARD GROUT

Working diagonally, spread grout across the tiled surface, pressing it into the gaps.

Drag a piece of dowelling along the gaps between tiles to produce an even finish.

EPOXY GROUT

Press long, thin strips of grout into the gaps with the edge of the applicator.

Rub along the edges with a soft, damp cloth. Always work in the same direction.

HOW TO TILE WALLS

A tiled wall is both beautiful and practical, and tiling a complete wall is not too difficult a job for the average handy person. However, if you have never done anything like this before, it is wise to begin with a simple and fairly small area such as a splashback, dado, etc. The secret of successful tiling lies in planning the job properly at the outset so that you can judge the effect before rushing out to buy boxes of tiles.

Always buy the best tools you can afford, and use and keep them safely – this applies for all do-it-yourself jobs. Before starting, make sure you have all the materials to complete the job – i.e. enough tiles, adhesive, grout, etc. – nothing is more frustrating than running out of materials halfway through a job!

Setting Out the Tiles

A successful tiled wall is set out so a pattern is easy on the eye, centred on any features (e.g. a window, basin, stove recess, chimney breast, etc.) and not "slipping off the wall," and has a good pattern match. Tiles should not have to be awkwardly cut.

To achieve this usually means starting in the centre of a wall, or area to be tiled, and working out toward the edges with any cut pieces (of equal size) coming at the end of each row. This is fairly easy on a blank wall, but harder to achieve where there are projections, recesses or doors and windows to be accommodated.

Find the exact centre (midpoint) of the wall to be tiled by measuring and drawing a central vertical line

with the aid of a plumb line. Lay out a row of tiles as a "dry run," placing a tile on each side of this line. If it looks awkward and will result in difficult cuts at each end of the row of tiles, you could centre one tile on the midpoint. This is often the best

method when tiling splashbacks for a sink or behind the bath, centring a single tile on the midpoint behind the faucets.

Make a gauge or marking stick from a length of wood and mark it in the width of the tiles you are using. Hold it against the wall in various positions to see how the tiles fall. You can do this on both the horizontal and vertical plane, but you will have to make two different gauge sticks if the tiles are not square.

It is also essential to establish a level base – the bottom row of tiles must be level. This means working to the true horizontal, which may not necessarily be the same as the baseboard (skirting) or the floor! To get this right, draw a line right around the room with the aid of a batten and spirit level.

Alternatively, lightly tack a lath to the wall, approximately one tile high from the floor. The line should not be more than the depth of the tile above the finishing point, and a spare tile can be used to check this. If the

INITIAL PREPARATION

Use a plumb line (or weighted string) to find the true vertical line; use a spirit level to find the true horizontal line.

floor is uneven and the tiles will leave a gap, redraw the line or replace the lath. When tiling more than one wall, continue the line around the other walls, again checking with the spirit level at regular intervals.

If there are doors, windows, bathroom or kitchen appliances, pipes, etc., to be accommodated, figure out where the tiles will fall.

◀ Tiling around a window recess can be a very attractive and practical solution in a kitchen or bathroom where the window is above the sink. The simple geometric effect coordinates well with the pleated Roman shades used for the window.

TILING A WALL USING BATTENS

Mark the baseline on the wall. Drive nails partway through the wooden batten.

Place the batten level with the baseline and tap in the nails to hold it in place.

Figure out where the last whole tile will fall. Use a spirit level to mark this line.

Attach a vertical batten in place and then start tiling where the two battens intersect.

When complete, remove adhesive from between the battens and tiles with a knife.

Remove the battens. Measure and cut tiles to fit into the spaces that are left.

TILING CORNERS

Overlap one tile over the other at internal corners; choose the least noticeable way.

Finish external corners with a trim strip. Make sure the tiles on either side align.

TILING WINDOW RECESSES

Tile the wall before the recess. Arrange for equal size cuts at both ends of the sill.

Tile the underside of the recess last. Tape the tiles for extra support.

Use the marking stick to measure the tile widths between the baseline and any fixtures; if the tile cuts will fall awkwardly, adjust the baseline or midpoint accordingly. Try to line tiles up with window frames (so the sill can also be neatly tiled) and to come level with bathtubs, etc.

You can use squared paper to see how the tiles will fall. This is especially practical if the wall to be tiled has lots of features, or the pattern will be complicated to match. Make one square equal to one tile.

Installing the Tiles
If you are using self-spacing or "Universal" tiles, you do not need to use matchsticks or tile spacers, but they will be necessary if the tiles do not have special bevelled edges.

Use the recommended tile adhesive (a waterproof adhesive is essential for kitchens and bathrooms). Starting at the midpoint, spread the adhesive using a good notched spreader and lay the tiles in blocks of approximately 1 square yard/metre and work along the wall. (Start in a corner if the wall is blank and there are to be no tile cuts.) Use the back of the spreader to scoop the adhesive from the tub and spread it in an even layer 1/16in (2–3mm) thick, "combing" it with the notches on the spreader.

Start to set the tiles in place, aligning them with your batten or lath. If a sealing strip is to be positioned between a work surface (or bath) and the tiles, bed it into the adhesive before aligning the tiles with it. Push each tile firmly into position

on the adhesive, checking that it sits square with the aid of a plumb line and spirit level.

If you are using matchsticks or tile spacers, push these into the adhesive at the top and bottom of the tiles where they join. Complete the area, checking regularly that the tiles are square, level and flush. Continue until you have filled the area which can be covered with uncut tiles. Leave for 12–24 hours (or until the adhesive is dry) and then remove any laths and/or battens and pull out the spacers or matchsticks, reserving them for future use. Measure, cut and install tiles in the area around the edge of the tiling, or lay border tiles in position. When the adhesive has set, clean and grout the tiles.

HOW TO TILE A WORK SURFACE

Tiled countertops are a very practical finish for surfaces in the kitchen, bathroom, bedroom and children's rooms, and are relatively easy to install as the force of gravity is not working against you! For a seamless look, a single slab of granite, slate or marble can be used as a continuous top; but installation would be a job for the expert as its weight makes it difficult to handle.

A tiled top is also heavy, so first make sure the structure of the unit to be tiled is strong enough to take the weight. If necessary, reinforce the corner joints, backs and sides of kitchen, bedroom or bathroom units, or any other piece of furniture to be used, such as a chest of drawers, desk, table or washstand.

A tiled kitchen countertop will blunt knives and is not an ideal surface for rolling out pastry or for chopping food, but a chopping board or marble slab can be placed on top, or be inset into the surface. Decide the most practical and coolest position if it is to be integrated.

The edges of the tiled area can be finished with either edging tiles or wood. Edging tiles sometimes come as part of a standard work surface kit, complete with internal and external corner edge tiles. Hardwood may be chosen to link with units or furniture, or it could be coloured to contrast and provide an extra design feature. However you finish edges, make sure it will be possible to open the top drawer of the units!

Tiles for a work surface should be at least ¼in (5mm) thick to withstand hot and heavy pans. They should not be too highly glazed since this surface is slippery. Most wall tiles are not suitable for a kitchen countertop, although they could be used in a bathroom or bedroom. Select tiles to use from the choice of special ones available, or some of the thinner floor tiles are also suitable. The work surface and floor could be tiled to coordinate. When tiling over an old tiled countertop, thinner tiles can be used.

The size of tile you choose is also a matter of personal taste. The smaller

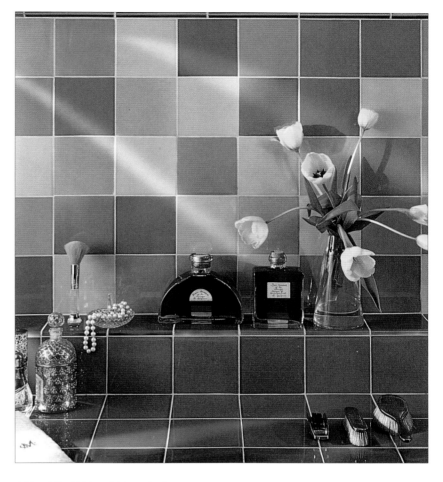

▲ The cool blues and greens create a "patchwork" effect on the splashback above the blue tiled work surface. The tiles line up well across the two surfaces.

(4½ x 4½in/108 x 108mm) tiles are more complicated to work with, and tiles over 6 x 6in (150 x 150mm) can be more difficult to handle and may need cutting. In the main, the size of the surface to be tiled will influence your decision since it is better to cover as much of the surface as possible with uncut tiles. It is also visually pleasing to have the continuity of the same tiles on the wall and forming a splashback or curved upstand.

It is essential to use the right adhesive and grout. The adhesive should be of the "thin-bed" floor type and the best grout to use is an "epoxy grout," which is impervious to cooking liquids and germs and should be relatively stain-resistant. This type of grout has to be applied with a spatula, rather than a sponge or squeegee.

A suitable, firm surface is needed to provide a "bed" for the tiles. Some cupboards may be covered already with wood or laminate which may be strong enough to tile over, but if necessary, screw supporting battens to the underside of the unit. Curved post-formed edges need to be cut square, or built up with wooden lipping and putty (filler). Metal edging should be removed; wooden lipping can either be tiled over or built up to form the edge of the new tiled work surface.

FINDING THE "KEY" TILE

Plan the layout of the tiles carefully. A "key" tile – where the horizontal and vertical rows intersect – will become obvious.

TILING A WORK SURFACE

If the edge of the work surface is to be trimmed with wood, nail a batten into position to act as a guide. The wooden trim should be attached after tiling is complete to avoid damaging it.

If the edge of the work surface is to be tiled, attach the ceramic edging first. Start with the "key" tile and make sure that the tiles on the work surface align exactly with those of the edging.

Spread adhesive over the work surface with a notched spreader. Do enough for about six tiles at a time.

Lay all of the whole tiles in place, separating them with spacers. Do not forget to put spacers between the tiles and the edging.

Press each row of tiles with a batten to ensure that they are level – check with a spirit level. Lift and relay wherever necessary – do not try to force the tiles into position.

TILING AWKWARD AREAS

Tile the work surface before the splashback. Tile right up to the wall and then allow the wall tiles to overlap those at the edge of the countertop.

Curved tiles can be used for a neat join between the wall and countertop.

Remove socket faceplates and trim the tile to fit the hole. Put the faceplate back in place after grouting.

Take out burners (hobs) and tile under the edges. Do not forget to switch off the power when doing this. Use wooden battens to support them until you have finished grouting.

Overlap tiles at outside edges in the least noticeable way. Usually, the horizontal tiles overlap the vertical ones.

If you are starting from scratch, for the base use a good-quality plywood or blockboard at least ½in (12mm) thick, or ¾in (19mm) chipboard. Both must be supported along the edges about every 24in (600mm) – try to relate the size of the boards to the module of the tiles. Before you position the board on the top of the unit, cut holes to accommodate the appliances, sink, etc.

The edges of equipment may overlap the tiled surface, which will involve some loosening, etc. This may also be necessary when fitting tiles around power sockets and switches (always make sure the electricity supply is turned off at the fuse box).

Back to the Drawing Board
If you are planning a kitchen from scratch, you need to figure out exactly where everything is to be sited. Consider the basic principles of kitchen planning and fit in the "work triangle" in the most practical and convenient way. Also think of safety aspects – do not position the sink

▷ Work surface tiles do not have to be laid at right angles to the edges of units or walls. Here, the tiles are laid diamond-fashion to create extra visual interest. Take care to ensure that the grout lines look right on the countertop where they meet the wall tiles.

FINDING THE MIDPOINT FOR A SPLASHBACK

Divide the length of the wall in two and use the edge of a tile as the midpoint.

Alternatively, it may look better to use the middle of a tile as the midpoint.

directly opposite the stove, or place the stove directly behind doors; it can also be dangerous to site the burners (hob) under a window.

When planning the layout of the work surface, it is best to make a scale plan to figure out exactly where the tiles and cuts will fall, and also to help you site the sink and other appliances. Use squared paper, making one tile equal to one or more squares – you can use squared paper even if the tiles are rectangular in shape. Aim for any cuts to be placed to the back of the units, and in the case of an L-shaped arrangement, make sure a whole tile meets its partner at the inner bend of the L, and that the joins are continuous along both surfaces.

Once you have the basic plan on paper, you can take it to the tile supplier and use it as a guide to purchase the right quantities. As with all tiling jobs, buy a few spare tiles to allow for mistakes!

Installing and Finishing
The method of installing tiles on a work surface is similar to that of wall or floor tiles. With the top in position, lay the tiles on the surface to make sure the plan is the most practical one. By doing this, a "key" tile will become evident, which is usually either centred on the surface or where the two extensions of the "L" meet. Draw around this tile on the surface to be tiled and use it as a guideline.

If you have opted for a ceramic tiled edge, install these tiles first; then work back towards the wall and sides with the main tiles, using the "key" tile as a guide. When tiling an edge, spread the adhesive on the back of the tile, not on the prepared surface. If you plan a wooden trim, this will be added later, but in the meantime, tack a piece of batten the same size as the trim along the edge of the work surface as a guide.

To tile the main area of the top, use a special notched spreader to spread enough adhesive to lay four to six tiles, ⅛in (2–3mm) thick. Push the tiles firmly into position, inserting spacers in between. Every so often, use a spirit level to check that the tiles are perfectly flush and level. Use a piece of batten to press the tiles down flat after laying an area of about four to six tiles, and if necessary, lift any which are standing out and relay them.

When the main tiles are laid, cut and lay any for the corners, for under the lip of inset fittings, or along the sides or back of the top. Lay upstanding edge tiles and any splashback tiles to be in line with the tiles on the work surface.

Clean the tiles and leave to harden for approximately 12–24 hours, and then apply the grout. Epoxy grout is sticky and different from conventional grout, and needs to be applied with a special applicator, following the manufacturer's instructions carefully.

SUPPLIERS

Amtico Company Ltd [AC]
Kingfield Road
Coventry CV6 5PL
(UK) 01203 861400

Karl Arnold [AN]
1 The Strand
Topsham
Exeter EX3 0JB
(UK) 01392 873427

Atkinson-Jones [AJ]
23 Sudeley Street
Kemp Town
Brighton
East Sussex BN2 1HE
(UK) 01273 673924

Acquisitions Fireplaces [AF]
4–6 Jamestown Road
London NW1 7BY
(UK) 0171 482 2949

Carreaux de Casbah [CC]
20 Wellington Lane
Montpelier
Bristol BS6 5PY
(UK) 01179 427318

Castelnau Tiles [CA]
175 Church Road
London SW13 9HR
(UK) 0181 741 2452

Ceramique Internationale [CI]
Unit 1, Royds Lane
Lower Wortley Road
Leeds LS12 6DU
(UK) 01132 310218

Chantecler Ceramics [CH]
Gwastod Bach
Llanpumpsaint
Dyfed
Wales SA33 6LH
(UK) 01559 384671

Chiswick Fireplace Co [CF]
68 Southfield Road

Chiswick
London W4 1BD
(UK) 0181 995 4011

Colour 1 Ceramics [C1]
412 Richmond Road
East Twickenham
Middlesex TW1 2EB
(UK) 0181 891 0691

Corres Mexican Tiles [CM]
29 Great Suffolk Road
London SE1 0NS
(UK) 0171 261 0941

Country Floors [CO]
8735 Melrose Avenue
Los Angeles CA 90069–5014
(US) 310 657 0510

Country Tile Design [CD]
Court Farm
Court Lane
Standerwick
(near Frome)
Somerset BA11 2PR
(UK) 01373 831381

Criterion Tiles [CT]
196 Wandsworth Bridge Road
London SW6 2UF
(UK) 0171 736 9610

Decorum Ceramic Studio [DC]
North's Estate
Piddington
High Wycombe
Bucks HP14 3BE
(UK) 01494 882299

Elon Ltd [EL]
5 Skyline Drive
Hawthorn NY 10532
(US) 914 347 7800

Elon Tiles [ET]
66 Fulham Road
London SW3 6HH
(UK) 0171 460 4600

Fired Earth [FE]
Twyford Mill
Oxford Road

Adderbury
Oxon OX17 3HP
(UK) 01295 812088

Hastings [HA]
230 Park Avenue South
New York 10003
(US) 212 674 9700

H&R Johnson [HR]
Highgate Tile Works
Tunstall
Stoke-on-Trent ST6 4JX
(UK) 01782 575575

Ideal Standard [IS]
The Bathroom Works
National Avenue
Kingston-upon-Hull HU5 4HF
(UK) 01482 346461

Ideal Tiles [IT]
2048 Broadway
70th Street
New York 10023
(US) 212 799 3600

Jaafar Design [JD]
78 Kingshill Road
Dursley
Gloucestershire GL11 4EF
(UK) 01453 547204

Jones's Tiles [JT]
Orleton Manor
Ludlow
Shropshire SY8 4HR
(UK) 01568 85666

Langley Architectural [LA]
161–167 Borough High Street
London SE1 1HU
(UK) 0171 407 4444

Life Enhancing Tile Co [LE]
Designs by Robert Manners
Unit 4a Alliance House
14 St Mary's Road
Portsmouth PO1 5PH
(UK) 01705 862709

Malbrook Conservatories [MC]
66 Upper Richmond Road

London SW15 2RP
(UK) 0181 875 1441

Marlborough Tiles [MT]
Elcot Lane
Marlborough
Wiltshire SN8 2AY
(UK) 01672 512422

Marston & Langinger [ML]
192 Ebury Street
London SW1E 8UP
(UK) 0171 823 6829

Merchant Tiler [ME]
Direct all enquiries to:
Fired Earth

Metropolitan Tile Co [MP]
Lower Audley Center
Kent Street
Blackburn
Lancashire BB1 1DE
(UK) 01254 695111

Minton Hollins [MH]
Direct all enquiries to:
H&R Johnson

Mira Showers [MS]
Cromwell Road
Cheltenham
Glouc GL52 5EP
(UK) 01242 221221

Steven Morgan [MO]
Jericho
Mells Down
Mells
Frome
Somerset BA11 2RL
(UK) 01373 813242

Mosaic Workshop [MW]
Unit B
443–449 Holloway Road
London N7 6LJ
(UK) 0171 263 2997

Danka Napiorkowska [NP]
14 Higher Bridge Park
St Matthews Hill
Wadebridge

Cornwall PL27 6UW
(UK) 01208 812024

Naturestone [NT]
Crossways, Silwood Road
Sunninghill
Ascot
Berkshire SL5 0PZ
(UK) 01344 27617

Oak Leaf Conservatories [OL]
Kettlestring Lane
Clifton Common
York YO3 8XF
(UK) 01904 690401
and
876 Davis Drive
Atlanta
Georgia 30327
(US) 800 360 6283

Quemere International [QU]
112 Franklin Avenue
Yonkers NY 10705
(US) 914 476 5950

Paris Ceramics [PC]
386 King's Road
Chelsea
London SW3 5UZ
(UK) 0171 351 3467

Pilkington Tiles Ltd [PT]
PO Box 4
Clifton Junction
Manchester M27 2LP
(UK) 0161 794 2024

Reject Tile Shop [RJ]
178 Wandsworth Bridge Road
London SW6 2UQ
(UK) 0171 731 6098

Reptile Tiles and Ceramics [RP]
Gwaith Menyn
Llanglydwen
Whitland
Dyfed
Wales SA34 0XP
(UK) 01994 419402

Robus Ceramics [RO]
Evington Park

Hastingleigh
Ashford
Kent TN25 5JH
(UK) 01233 750330

Rye Tiles [RT]
The Old Brewery
Wishyard
Rye
Sussex TN31 7DH
(UK) 01797 223038

Ann Sacks [AS]
5 East 16th Street
New York 10003
(US) 212 463 0492

Sally Anderson Ceramics [SA]
Parndon Mill
Harlow
Essex CM20 2HP
(UK) 01279 420982

Shelly [SH]
979 Third Avenue
New York 10022
(US) 212 832 2255

T&C Sloper Medieval Tiles [SL]
6 Grovesnor Terrace
Bear Street
Barnstuple
Devon EX32 7DS
(UK) 01271 77403

Société Carré [SC]
9 rue de Pierre de Geyter
Pierrefitte 93380
France
(FR) 48 26 22 63

Stonell [SN]
Unit 1
Bockingfold
Goudhurst
Kent TN17 2AH
(UK) 01580 211167

Sunny McLean & Co [SU]
3800 NE 2nd Avenue
Miami
Florida 33137
(US) 305 573 5943

Sussex Terracotta [ST]
Nye Road
Burgess Hill
West Sussex RH15 0LZ
(UK) 01444 241236

Terra Firma [TF]
70 Chalk Farm Road
London NW1 8AN
(UK) 0171 485 7227

Tile Art [TA]
45 Distons Lane
Chipping Norton
Oxon OX7 5NY
(UK) 01608 643028

Tiles and Flooring [TI]
175 Muswell Hill Broadway
Muswell Hill
London N10 3RS
(UK) 0181 883 8879

The Tile Shop [TS]
4–6 Chamberlayne Road
London NW10 3JD
(UK) 0181 968 9497

Tiles of Stow [TW]
Lanston Priory Workshops
Station Road
Kingham
Oxon OX7 6UP
(UK) 01608 658951

Tile with Style [TY]
270 Kentish Town Road
London NW5 2AA
(UK) 0171 485 9455

Topps Tile Kingdom [TT]
Telephone all enquiries to:
(UK) 01162 750336

Tower Ceramics Ltd [TC]
91 Parkway
Camden Town
London NW1 7PP
(UK) 0171 485 7192

Twyfords Bathrooms [TB]
Lawton Road
Alsager

Stoke-on-Trent ST7 2DF
(UK) 01207 879777

WD Virtue Co Inc [WD]
PO Box 126
160 Broad Street
Summit NJ 07901
(US) 908 273 6936

Whichford Pottery [WF]
Whichford
Shipston-on-Stour
Warwickshire CV36 5PG
(UK) 01608 684833

Wickes Ltd [WI]
120–138 Station Road
Harrow
Middlesex HA1 2QB
(UK) 0181 901 2000

Bronwyn Williams-Ellis [WL]
Old Orchard
88a Walcot Street
Bath
Avon BA1 5BD
(UK) 01225 460805

Winchester Tile Company [WT]
Unit C1, Pegasus Court
Ardglen Road
Whitchurch
Hampshire RG28 7BP
(UK) 01256 896922

World's End Tiles [WE]
BR Yard
Silverthorne Road
Battersea
London SW8 3HE
(UK) 0171 720 8358

Anna Wyner [WY]
2 Ferry Road
London SW13 9RX
(UK) 0181 748 3940

Mary Rose Young [YO]
Oak House
Arthur's Folly
Parkend, Lydney
Gloucestershire GL15 4JQ
(UK) 01594 563425

GLOSSARY

Accent colours: small amounts of colour introduced to add interest or balance to a scheme.

Advancing colours: "warm" colours in the spectrum which appear to come forward, making a space seem more cosy, but smaller.

Border tiles: narrow strips of material used to decorate or edge a wall area; usually curved and may have a raised design and protrude like a nosing; used above a part-tiled wall or dado to finish.

Carrés: literally "squares;" name given to natural terracotta slabs, usually from the Mediterranean.

Ceramic: a heat-resistant material made by firing or baking clay.

Chair rail: see Dado rail.

Clay: natural product taken from the earth and fired in kilns (or sometimes sunbaked) to make tiles; can be coloured (red or earth tones) or white (china); for terra clay see Earthenware.

Colour values: weight or strength of colour, sometimes called tone.

Complementary colours: contrasting "opposite" colours; those which face each other on a colour wheel; create a stimulating effect.

Crackle glaze: when characteristic imperfections in the glaze produce an "antique" effect; such tiles should not be used on work surfaces or shower walls where an impervious surface is required.

Dado: lower area of wall between dado rail and baseboard (skirting); traditionally wood-panelled or covered with heavily textured wallcovering and painted; may be tiled to provide a practical surface to withstand knocks.

Dado rail: also called a chair rail; a wooden beading or plaster moulding mounted about 3ft (90cm) from the floor; can also be tiled; originally devised to prevent the backs of chairs from damaging fabric-hung walls; provides a convenient boundary between different wall treatments.

Drop-ins: small tiles which are combined with larger tiles to form a geometric pattern; mostly found in floor tiles; see Insets.

Earthenware: a type of coarse clay used for tiles and pottery.

Encaustic tiles: from the Greek for "burnt in;" an ancient method of producing inlaid tiles used in medieval monasteries and churches; the inlay process permanently fuses the pattern into the tile; characteristic colours are terracotta/black/beige (sometimes accented in blue).

Faience (Fayence): tin-enamelled earthenware made in Europe in 16th–18th centuries.

Field tiles: usually plain-coloured or slightly textured tiles intended for the major wall or floor area, but can be combined with patterned insets.

Glaze: a vitrified coating which makes tiles non-porous; added in liquid form before firing; the heat of the kiln produces a high gloss, although different types, such as matt, are also common.

Insets: see Drop-ins; can also refer to borders or pictorial tiles set into a plain floor or wall of field tiles.

Liner tiles: see Border tiles.

Lustre: rich, fluid, iridescent sheen on the surface of some wall tiles which looks like an oilslick; created by mixing a thin film made from metallic salts with the glaze.

Majolica: a process where a slip of white clay applied to the surface of a tile highlights the coloured glaze used in the final decoration; brought to Italy by Majorcan sailors c.1400.

Mosaics: small pieces of fired clay, glass or marble used to make a decorative pattern for floors and walls.

Motif: the dominant feature in a design, usually repeated regularly.

Mural: a picture or panel made from a combination of tiles.

Nosing: a type of border tile used to finish an area of tiling; often stands out in relief.

Onglaze: a method of glazing a predecorated tile with clear glaze so the pattern shows through.

Picture rail: simple beading running around walls below the cornice; pictures can be suspended by means of hooks and wires.

Receding colours: colours from the "cool" end of the spectrum; appear to go away into the distance, so creating an impression of space.

Relief tiles: tiles with a raised design, creating a 3D effect, usually made by using a mould.

Repeat: full length of a vertical design taken from one point to the next point where it repeats itself exactly; single tiles can form a repeat, although geometric patterns usually rely on several tiles.

Silk-screen printing: a method of producing a pattern by squeezing glaze, dye or pigment through an etched screen onto the surface.

Slate: a type of natural quarried material suitable for indoor and outdoor use; often riven (roughened) to make it non-slip.

Slipware: made by combining clay with water; more usually white clay and water mixed to the consistency of cream, used to cover red clay to enhance and highlight the final decoration.

Stoneware: made by combining clay with flint or silica to produce a material which can withstand very high firing temperatures, creating tiles suitable for exterior use in intense weather conditions.

Terracotta: from the Latin meaning "fired earth;" normally used to describe unglazed earthenware – a low-fired red clay used for tiles and pottery; also used to describe a deep burnt-orange (natural clay) colour.

Tesserae: individual units in a tessellated pavement; also used for geometric patterned tiles.

Tessellated pavement: floor made of hard-wearing mosaics set into a pattern – usually pictorial.

Tin glaze: glaze created by adding tin oxide to a lead glaze to produce a white opaque effect when fired.

Tint: a pale value of a colour made by adding white to a pure hue.

Tone: a middle value or colour made by adding grey to a pure hue.

Trompe l'oeil: literally to "deceive the eye;" method used to create a 3D effect on a flat plane or to simulate a view on a blank area of wall.

INDEX

Page numbers in *italics* refer to captions and illustrations

CREDITS

Quarto would like to thank all the tile manufacturers and retailers who so kindly supplied tiles and transparencies for use in this book.

We would also like to thank the following New York showrooms for generously allowing us to photograph many of their tiles: Ann Sacks, Country Floors, Elon Ltd, Ideal Tiles and Shelly.

We would particularly like to thank both Mary Rose Young and Ann Sacks for their kind assistance and cooperation throughout the production of this book.

Jacket (*clockwise from top left*):
Tile Art, Tiles of Stow, Aquisitions Fireplaces, Criterion Tiles, Sally Anderson Ceramics, Winchester Tile Co, Jaafar Design, Aquisitions Fireplaces, Reptile Tiles and Ceramics, Reject Tile Shop (centre)

In the following credits, each tile supplier is identified by a two-letter code (see Suppliers on pages 156–7 for full details).

a above; *m* middle (row); *b* below;
l left; *r* right; *c* centre

1 MW / 2–3 MW / 4–5 MW / 7 LA / 8 HA *al, ac*; CO *ar*; AS *bl*; FE *br* / 9 WI *al*; CO *ar*; HA *bl*; MH *bc*; LE *mr*; YO *br* / 13 PC / 14 FE / 15 PC *al*; HR *ac*; SC *mr*; CO *bl*; CM *br* / 16 CO *l*; DC *r* / 17 AS *l, br*; ME *ar* / 19 PC / 20 AS / 21 AS *a*; FE *b* / 22 CO / 23 CF *al, cl, r* / 24 FE / 25 AS *l*; CO *ar, br* / 27 HR / 28 DC / 29 FE *ac, ar, br* / 30 CO / 31 WE *al*; HR *ar*; AS *b* / 32 NT / 33 CO *a*; SN *b* / 34 AS / 35 OL *a*; FE *b* / 37 ST / 38 PC *a, b* / 39 CM / 40 PC *l*; CO *r* / 41 MC *l*; SN *r* / 42 WI *a*; MC *bc*; PC *br* / 43 HR / 45 HR / 46 CO / 47 MW *a*; SC *b* / 48 IS / 49 AS *l*; FE *r* / 50 IS *a*; CM *b* / 51 IS / 52 AS *l*; CO *r* / 53 SC / 54–55 *Tiles for Colour Directory section opener supplied by* AF, WL, CM, CT, EL, HA, JD, LE, MO, MT, YO, RP, RJ, SA, SU, SL, TY, WI / 57 SC / 58–59 *Tiles for Red*

Directory opener supplied by CO, CT, FE, MT, YO, RJ, SU, TC, TS, TY, WD, WT / 60 HR *l*; SC *r* / 61 AS *l*; MS *r* / 62 CM *al*; CC *ar*; SH *ml*; EL *mc*; CO *bl, bc, br* / 63 HA *al, ac, ar, ml, bl, br*; CO *mr*; CC *bc* / 64 EL *al*; IT *acl*; SH *acr*; AS *ar, br*; HA *ml, bl*; CO *mc* / 65 CO *al*; SH *ac*; IT *ar*; AS *mr, bcl, br*; RT *bl, bcr* / 66 AS *al, bc*; MH *ar*; SH *ml, mc*; CO *br* / 67 AS *al, ml, bl, bcr*; CO *acl*; HA *acr, mr*; SH *ar*; CC *bcl*, ET *br* / 68 SH *al, ar*; AS *ac, ml, mc*; IT *bl*; CO *bc*; EL *br* / 69 AS *al, bl*; AF *ac*; HA *ar, bcl*; AJ *ml*; RT *mr*; EL *bcr*; YO *br* / 70–71 *Tiles for Orange Directory opener supplied by* WL, CM, EL, FE, LE, MO, SL, TS, SU, TY / 72 SC *l*; C1 *r* / 73 BB *a*; CM *b* / 74 HA *al*; CM *ac*; SA *ar*; IT *mc*; CI *mr*; CO *bl*; CM *bc*; CC *br* / 75 HA *al*; CM *ac, bl*; HA *ar*; ML *mc*; AS *bcl*; ET *bcr*; ST *br* / 76 CM *al, ac, ml; mc, bl, bc, br*; TF *ar* / 77 HA *al*; CO *ac*; AS *ar, ml, mcl, mr, bcr, br*; ST *mcr*; CM *bl; bcl* / 78 *Tiles for Yellow Directory opener supplied by* WL, CM, MT, TY, WT / 80 WT *l*; PC *r* / 81 CM *l*; MW *r* / 82 JT *al*; AJ *ac*; WE *ar*; CD *ml*; DC *bc, br* / 83 FE *al*; CM *acl, mc*; AS *acr, ar, ml, bc*; WE *mr*; TS *bl*; YO *br* / 84 CO *al, ar, ml*; EL *acl*; HA *mcl*; SH *mcr*; JT *mcr*; DC *bc, br* / 85 CD *al*; FE *ar*; TF *mc*; CM *mr*; HA *bl, bc*; YO *br* / 86–87 *Tiles for Green Directory opener supplied by* AF, CM, CT, EL, JD, LE, RJ, SA, TA, TC, TW, TY, WT / 88 HR / 89 HR *l*; AS *ar*; SC *br* / 90 ET *al, acl, mcl*; EL *acr, ar, mcr*; MP *ml*; CM *mr*; YO *bl*; HR *bc*; ET *br* / 91 CO *al*; HR *acl*; AS *acr, ar, mcr, mr, bc*; EL *ml*; HA *mcl, bl*; ET *br* / 92 CO *al, acl, ml, br*; CM *acr*; CC *ar, mc*; SC *bl*; RT *bc* / 93 CM *al*; SH *ac, mr*; CO *ar*; ET *ml*; CC *bl, bc*; AS *br* / 94 HA *al*; SA *ac*; DC *ar*; CD *mcl*; CH *mcr*; TW *bl*; JT *bcl*; AS *bcr*; SH *br* / 95 AF *al*; HA *acl*; AS

acr; CO *ar*; PC *mcr*; TW *mr*; AS *bl, bcl, bcr, br* / 96 AS *al, ac, ar, ml, mr, bl, bcr*; HA *bcl*; SH *br* / 97 CO *al, acl, ml, bl, bc*; SH *acr, bcl*; AS *ar, bcr, br*; HA *mc* / 98–99 *Tiles for Blue Directory opener supplied by* WL, CM, JD, LE, MO, MT, RJ, SA, TW, TY, WT, WF / 100 HR / 101 FE *l*; AN *ar*; SA *br* / 102 HA *al, mcl*; AS *ac, bl, bc*; CO *ar*, ET *br* / 103 HA *al, bl*; AS *acl, acr, bcr, mc*; IT *ar*; HR *mr*; CM *bcl*; SH *br* / 104 AS *al, acl, ar, mr, bcr, br*; CO *acr*; WT *ml*; CM *mcl*; HA *bcl* / 105 RT *al*; AS *ac, ar, bl*; CO *ml, mr*; CM *mcr, bcl*; HA *bcr, br* / 106 CM *al*; CO *acl, ar, mr*; AJ *acr*; SH *ml, bl*; AS *bc*; CA *br* / 107 IT *al*; AJ *ar*; SH *mcr, bcr*; CH *mr*; AS *bl, bcl*; IT *br* / 108 AS *al, ml, mc, mr*; WT *ac*; SH *ar*; DC *bl*; CO *bc*; NP *br* / 109 SH *al, mr*; DC *ac*; CO *ar, br*; FE *ml*; AS *bl*; IT *bcl*; TW *bcr* / 110–111 *Tiles for Neutral and Natural Directory opener supplied by* CM, EL, LE, FE, RJ, SA, TC, TS / 112 AS *l*; HR *r* / 113 AS *l, r* / 114 HA *al, bl*; AS *ac, ar*; HR *ml*; ML *mr*; SH *br* / 115 CO *al, ac, bc*; HR *ar, br*; AS *mc*; WT *bl* / 116 CO *al, ar, ml, mr*; ET *acl*; MW *acr*; EL *bl, bc*; AS *br* / 117 CO *al, acl, bl, bcl, bcr*; SH *acr, ml, mcr*; CM *acr*; AS *mr, br* / 118 PC *al*; SH *acl*; HA *ar, bl, br*; AS *ml, mcl, mcr, mr*; CO *bc* / 119 AS *al, ac, mr, br*; SH *ar*; CO *mc, bl, bc* / 120 EL *al*; HA *acl*; ML *acr*; AS *ar, ml, mcr, mr, bc*; CO *bl, br* / 121 AS *al, ac, ar, mc, mr, br*; CO *bl, bc* / 122–123 *Tiles for Black and White Directory opener supplied by* EL, FE, LE, MW, QU, RJ, TI, TC, TW, TY, WT / 124 TT *l*; AS *r* / 125 CO *l*; AS *r* / 126 HA *al, br*; AS *acl, acr, ar, mcl, mcr*; CO *mr, bl*; EL *bc* / 127 HA *al, ar*; AS *ac*; CO *ml*; EL *bl, br* / 128 AS *al, ac, bl, bc, br*; SH *ar, ml* / 129 HA *al*; SH *ac, mcl, bc*; TW *ar, br*; AS *mcr*; CM *mr*; IT *bl* / 130 LE *al, ml*; CO *acl, ar, mcl, mr*; WE *acr*; HA *bl, bc, br* / 131 CO *al, bl*; HA *ar, bc*; AS *mc, mr*; YO *br* / 132 *Tiles for Metallic Directory opener supplied by* CO, HA, JT, YO, SU, TS, WD / 133 AS *l, r* / 134 CO *al, ml*; AS *ac, bl, bc, br*; HA *ar* / 135 HA *al*; AS *ac, mc, bc*; CO *ar, bl, br* / 136–137 *Tiles for Practical Pointers opener supplied by* FE, LE; *Tools supplied by* TC / 138 HR *a*; FE *b* / 139 LA *l* FE *r* / 142 CA *a*; ST *b* / 144 WE / 145 MP / 146 AC / 149 SC / 150 CM / 151 MT / 153 SC / 155 AS / 160 MW

All other photographs are the copyright of Quarto.